Data:

Fuel for Artificial Neurons:

How Information Powers Intelligent Machines

by

Susie Hala

IntelliGloss

AI Education Series

Legal Disclaimer

Educational Purpose Disclaimer

"This publication is part of the IntelliGloss AI Education Series, a structured curriculum support system for AI literacy in grades 6–12."

The information presented in this publication is provided for educational and informational purposes only. This book is intended to support educators, administrators, parents, and learners in understanding the concepts, opportunities, and challenges associated with artificial intelligence in education. It is not intended to serve as legal, technical, policy, cybersecurity, or professional advice.

Readers should consult qualified professionals, institutional guidelines, and local regulations before implementing any educational programs, technologies, or policies described in this book.

Technology and Accuracy Disclaimer
Artificial intelligence is a rapidly evolving field. While every effort has been made to ensure the accuracy and reliability of the information presented at the time of publication, technologies, policies, research findings, and best practices may change over time. The author and publisher make no guarantees that all information will remain current or applicable in future technological environments.

Readers are encouraged to verify tools, platforms, and recommendations independently before using them in educational settings.

Implementation Responsibility
Schools, educators, and institutions are solely responsible for determining how and whether to implement artificial intelligence tools, strategies, or classroom activities discussed in this book. Educational environments vary widely, and policies regarding technology use, student privacy, and curriculum development differ by district, state, and country.

The author and publisher assume no responsibility for outcomes resulting from the implementation of ideas, examples, or frameworks described in this book.

Student Safety and Data Privacy
Artificial intelligence tools may involve the collection or processing of data. Educators and institutions are responsible for ensuring that any technology used complies with applicable student privacy laws, data protection regulations, and school policies, including but not limited to FERPA, COPPA, GDPR, or other relevant regulations depending on jurisdiction.

The author and publisher are not responsible for the privacy practices, security policies, or data handling procedures of third-party platforms or software mentioned in this book.

Third-Party Tools and References
This book may reference third-party technologies, organizations, research studies, or platforms
for illustrative and educational purposes. Such references do not constitute endorsements or
guarantees regarding the performance, reliability, safety, or suitability of those tools for
educational use.

Educators and institutions should conduct their own evaluations and risk assessments before
adopting any technology.

No Professional Liability
The author and publisher shall not be held liable for any direct, indirect, incidental, or
consequential damages resulting from the use or misuse of the information contained in this
book. This includes but is not limited to decisions related to curriculum design, technology
adoption, classroom instruction, institutional policies, or educational outcomes.

Educational Interpretation
The concepts and examples provided in this book are intended to support discussion and
learning. They should not be interpreted as official standards, mandatory guidelines, or
universally applicable policies for artificial intelligence education.

Schools and educators are encouraged to adapt the ideas presented here according to their local
policies, cultural context, educational standards, and student needs.

Author's Intent
The goal of this book is to promote responsible AI literacy, thoughtful discussion, and ethical
awareness as schools prepare students for a world increasingly shaped by intelligent
technologies.

The author encourages readers to approach artificial intelligence education with curiosity,
caution, and a commitment to responsible learning.

Title: Data: Fuel for Artificial Neurons How Information Powers Intelligent Machines

ISBN: 978-1-972925-06-5

This book is intended for educational and informational purposes. Artificial intelligence
technologies and policies evolve rapidly, and the author makes no guarantee regarding the

completeness, accuracy, or continued applicability of the information presented. Educators, schools, and institutions are responsible for evaluating and implementing technologies in accordance with their own policies, legal requirements, and educational standards.

Dedication

This book is dedicated to the next generation of learners—
the students who will grow up in a world shaped by intelligent technology,
and who deserve to understand it with clarity, confidence, and purpose.

To the educators who show up every day with dedication and heart,
guiding students through a rapidly changing world—
your role has never been more important.

To the parents and families who support learning at home,
encouraging curiosity, responsibility, and growth—
you are the foundation of every child's success.

And to my granddaughters,
whose curiosity, imagination, and future inspire me to do this work—
this book is for you.

May you not only learn how to use technology,
but understand it, question it, and shape it for the good of others.

About the Author

Susie Hala
Founder of the IntelliGloss AI Education Series

Susie Hala is an author, educator, and curriculum developer dedicated to advancing artificial intelligence literacy in education. Her work focuses on helping schools, educators, and students understand how intelligent technologies are shaping modern society—and why that understanding is essential for the next generation.

Hala is the creator of the IntelliGloss AI Education Series, a comprehensive and growing collection of educational books designed to make complex artificial intelligence concepts accessible, structured, and practical for classroom use. Her work emphasizes clarity, organization, and responsible implementation, enabling schools to introduce AI literacy without requiring advanced technical backgrounds.

In addition to her work in education, Hala brings hands-on experience working with artificial intelligence systems, including early exposure to rule-based AI technologies during her time working with AT&T. She has also developed modern digital platforms that integrate artificial intelligence, automation, and online systems, building e-commerce solutions and AI-driven applications that connect payment platforms, hosting environments, and conversational AI tools into real-world, functional systems.

This combination of foundational understanding and practical experience allows her to translate complex AI concepts into clear, accessible language for both educators and students.

Recognizing that artificial intelligence is rapidly transforming how information is created, interpreted, and used, Hala advocates for equipping students with the ability not only to use AI tools, but to understand, question, and evaluate them. Her work emphasizes critical thinking, ethical awareness, and responsible digital citizenship.

The IntelliGloss AI Education Series supports schools in teaching key areas such as artificial intelligence foundations, algorithms, machine learning concepts, and AI ethics, as well as the broader evolution of intelligent systems—from Artificial Narrow Intelligence (ANI) to Artificial General Intelligence (AGI) and Artificial Superintelligence (ASI). These resources are designed for students in grades 6–12 and for educators seeking structured, classroom-ready approaches to AI literacy.

In addition to her work in education publishing, Hala has a strong background in entrepreneurship, having built and managed multiple businesses and educational initiatives. Her experience across industries reinforces her belief that technology education must remain grounded in human values, critical thinking, and ethical responsibility.

Her mission is clear: to ensure that the next generation understands intelligent technology—not just how to use it, but how it truly works.

Preface

Two Students. Two Paths. One Future.

Before we begin, it is important to understand why learning how artificial intelligence works—not just how to use it—matters for every student.

Imagine two students who have just graduated from high school and are preparing for a job interview. The first student knows how to use artificial intelligence tools. This student can generate answers, complete assignments quickly, and rely on AI to assist with tasks. However, this student does not understand how artificial intelligence works behind the scenes.

The second student also knows how to use AI tools, but in addition, understands the foundational concepts behind them. This student has learned about data, algorithms, tokens, models, and how intelligent systems are trained and operate. This student can think critically about AI, recognize its limitations, and adapt when needed.

At first, the first student may appear faster and more efficient. However, over time, the second student demonstrates a deeper level of understanding, independence, and problem-solving ability. The second student is not only able to use artificial intelligence but also to question it, improve it, and grow with it.

This book is written for the second student.

In a world where artificial intelligence is becoming part of everyday life, students must not only learn how to use intelligent systems—they must learn how they work. True understanding leads to confidence, responsibility, and the ability to lead in an AI-driven future.

This perspective is not just theoretical—it is personal.

There was a time when I was the first student.

I knew how to use systems. I followed processes, completed tasks, and worked within structured environments that required accuracy and consistency. At the time, I did not think of these systems as artificial intelligence. They were simply part of the job—tools that had to be learned, followed, and mastered.

But looking back, I now understand something much deeper. I was working within rule-based systems—the earliest foundation of what we now recognize as artificial intelligence.

That realization changed everything.

As I began studying modern AI, including machine learning, deep learning, and intelligent systems, I started to see a clear connection between the past and the present. The structured systems I once worked in, the logic behind decision-making, and the step-by-step processes all still exist today. They have simply evolved.

Artificial intelligence did not appear overnight. It grew from rule-based systems into systems that can now learn, adapt, and assist in ways we never imagined.

I made a decision to move from simply using systems to understanding them.

That journey—from student one to student two—is the reason these books exist.

My mission is to help others bridge that same gap.

I believe that artificial intelligence should be understandable for everyone. It should not feel intimidating or out of reach. Students should feel confident exploring it. Teachers should feel prepared to introduce it. Everyday learners should have access to clear, structured explanations that make sense.

You do not need a background in technology. You do not need to know how to code. You only need the right explanation.

A Note from the Author

AI Is a Tool — Not a Decision Maker

Artificial Intelligence is becoming part of everyday life. Students use it to complete assignments, teachers use it to support instruction, and businesses use it to improve efficiency. While these tools are powerful and useful, there is an important truth that must remain clear from the very beginning:

Artificial Intelligence does not make decisions—people do.

One of the main purposes of this book is to help readers understand how AI works, what it can do, and—just as importantly—what it cannot do. AI systems are designed to process information, identify patterns, and generate responses based on data. They can assist with thinking, but they do not think independently. They can provide answers, but they do not understand consequences. They can suggest ideas, but they do not choose actions.

Every outcome that involves AI begins and ends with human involvement. A person asks the question. A person reviews the response. A person decides what to do next. Responsibility does not transfer to the machine.

In today's world, it is easy to confuse speed with intelligence and automation with authority. Because AI can respond quickly and confidently, it may appear as though it is making decisions. In reality, it is performing a task based on patterns it has learned—not exercising judgment.

This distinction matters. When people begin to rely on AI without understanding its role, they risk misunderstanding information, misusing technology, or placing trust in a system that is not capable of accountability. Clear understanding leads to responsible use.

This book was written to remove confusion and provide clarity. It is designed to help students and educators move beyond simply using AI tools and begin understanding the structure behind them. By learning how AI supports human thinking—rather than replacing it—readers can approach technology with confidence, awareness, and responsibility.

Artificial Intelligence is a powerful assistant. It can enhance learning, support creativity, and improve productivity. But it remains a tool.

The decisions, the actions, and the responsibility will always belong to the human.

— Susie Hala

Bringing Clarity to Artificial Intelligence

During a recent meeting with a school district, it became clear that one of the biggest challenges in artificial intelligence education is not the technology itself—but the way it is explained.

In that discussion, terms such as **chatbots, generative AI, agentic AI, autonomy, tools, hallucinations, and AI usage levels** were all mentioned together. While each term represents a distinct concept, they were often blended into one conversation without clear distinctions. The result was confusion, even among those who were actively trying to understand and make informed decisions.

This experience revealed an important truth:
Without clear definitions and structure, artificial intelligence becomes difficult to teach, difficult to learn, and difficult to use responsibly.

This book is designed to provide that structure.

Understanding the Core Concepts

To build a strong foundation, it is essential to separate and define the key ideas that are often confused.

Chatbot
A chatbot is a conversational interface that allows users to interact with an AI system through questions and prompts. It responds to input but does not act beyond what is directly requested.

Generative AI (Gen AI)
Generative AI refers to systems that create new content, including text, images, audio, and code.

These systems generate outputs based on patterns learned from large datasets. While powerful, generative AI does not truly understand information and may occasionally produce inaccurate results.

Agentic AI

Agentic AI describes systems that can take action toward a goal. Rather than responding to a single prompt, these systems can plan, make decisions within defined limits, and carry out multi-step tasks. This introduces a higher level of functional independence.

Autonomy

Autonomy refers to how independently an AI system operates. Some systems require constant human guidance, while others can perform multiple steps with minimal input. Autonomy is not a separate type of AI, but a measure of how much control the system has in completing tasks.

Additional Terms That Shape Understanding

AI Tools

AI tools are the applications people use to interact with artificial intelligence, such as writing assistants, design platforms, and data analysis systems. These tools make AI accessible in everyday tasks.

Hallucination

A hallucination occurs when an AI system generates information that appears correct but is inaccurate or unsupported. This is a known limitation of generative systems and highlights the need for human verification.

The AI Use Continuum

Another important concept is how AI is used at different levels. Rather than viewing AI as a single capability, it is more accurate to understand it as a continuum of use:

Assistive Use

AI supports simple tasks such as answering questions, correcting grammar, or providing suggestions.

Augmented Use

AI helps expand human capability by generating ideas, organizing content, and assisting in problem-solving.

Agentic Use

AI begins to take on multi-step responsibilities, planning and completing tasks with reduced human input.

This continuum shows that AI can range from a helpful assistant to a more independent system, depending on how it is applied.

The Moment Everything Sounded Like One Conversation

During a recent discussion on artificial intelligence, I listened closely as different experts spoke about the future of AI. One referenced advanced systems beyond human intelligence, another discussed goal-driven AI systems, and the conversation shifted quickly between topics like autonomy, tools, and system behavior. At first, it sounded like a single, unified discussion. But the more I listened, the more I realized something important.

They were not all talking about the same thing.

One part of the conversation focused on future possibilities—high-level systems that do not yet exist. Another part focused on current technologies that are already being used today. At the same time, different terms were being used to describe how AI behaves, how it makes decisions, and how much independence it may have. These ideas were layered together in a way that made them sound connected, even when they were not.

This experience revealed a major challenge in understanding artificial intelligence today. Many discussions combine different types of AI, different levels of intelligence, and different behaviors into one conversation. Without clear structure, these ideas begin to blur together. For someone trying to learn, this can feel overwhelming and confusing.

This book is built to solve that problem.

Artificial intelligence is not one single concept. It is a system made up of multiple layers. Some layers describe how intelligent a system is. Other layers describe how the system behaves. Still others describe how much control or independence the system has. When these layers are separated and explained clearly, AI becomes much easier to understand.

The goal of this book is to bring clarity where confusion often exists. Instead of mixing everything into one explanation, each concept is presented in a structured and organized way. This allows students, educators, and readers to see how the pieces fit together without losing sight of what each part actually means.

Understanding artificial intelligence begins with understanding its structure.

Once that structure is clear, the conversation becomes clearer as well.

Why Clarity Matters

When these concepts are not clearly defined, they merge into what can be described as a "conceptual blur." This can lead to misunderstandings about what AI can and cannot do, as well as unrealistic expectations or misuse in educational settings.

Clear understanding helps ensure that:

Students remain active learners, not passive users

Educators maintain control over instructional outcomes

AI is used as a support tool rather than a replacement for thinking

The Purpose of This Book

This book is built on a simple but essential principle:

Students should not only use artificial intelligence—they should understand it.

By clearly defining core concepts such as chatbots, generative AI, agentic AI, autonomy, and the continuum of AI use, this curriculum provides a structured pathway for developing both technical understanding and critical thinking.

Artificial intelligence is not a single tool or system. It is a collection of capabilities that must be understood in context.

Clarity is the foundation of responsible innovation.

Structuring Artificial Intelligence to Create Clarity and Understanding

Why Structure Is Necessary

Artificial intelligence is often presented as one unified concept. In many discussions, different ideas such as intelligence level, system behavior, and autonomy are combined into a single explanation. This can make AI appear more complex and confusing than it actually is.

Clarity begins when these ideas are separated and organized.

Structuring artificial intelligence allows each concept to be understood on its own before being connected to the larger system.

The Problem Without Structure

When AI is not structured, conversations may include multiple terms that sound related but describe entirely different things. For example, a discussion may move quickly between advanced future systems, current tools, and system behaviors without clearly distinguishing between them.

This creates the impression that all forms of AI operate at the same level and in the same way, which is not accurate.

Without structure, understanding becomes difficult.

The Solution: A Structured Approach

Artificial intelligence becomes clearer when it is organized into distinct categories.

Level explains how intelligent a system is.
Behavior explains how the system operates.
Control explains how much independence the system has.

Each category answers a different question. Together, they form a complete picture of how AI systems function.

Clarity Through Separation

A system can operate at a current level of intelligence while demonstrating different behaviors or levels of independence. For example, a system that generates responses and a system that takes steps toward completing a task may operate at the same intelligence level but differ in how they behave.

This distinction becomes clear only when structure is applied.

Instructional Insight

When teaching artificial intelligence, it is important to avoid presenting all concepts at once. Separating ideas into categories allows learners to focus on one dimension at a time, building understanding step by step.

Structured learning leads to deeper comprehension.

Key Takeaway

Artificial intelligence is not one single idea. It is a system made up of multiple parts. Structuring those parts creates clarity, improves understanding, and allows learners to see how the system truly works.

Reflection Question

How does separating intelligence level, behavior, and control make artificial intelligence easier to understand?

The IntelliGloss Instructional Approach

The IntelliGloss AI Education Series is designed to help students move beyond simply using AI tools and begin understanding artificial intelligence as a complete system.

Students learn how AI is built, how it operates, and how it connects to the real world.

A Message to Students and Readers

If you have ever felt that technology was too complicated…
If you have ever been confused by systems that were never clearly explained…

I want you to know:

You are capable of understanding artificial intelligence.

Sometimes, the challenge is not the concept itself—it is how it has been presented.

This series was created to change that.

A Message to Educators

To the educators using this material:

These books are designed to support you in introducing artificial intelligence in a way that is clear, structured, and meaningful for students.

AI is becoming part of every industry, and students deserve more than just exposure to tools—they deserve understanding.

This series aims to provide that foundation.

Final Reflection

Every experience we have—especially the challenging ones—prepares us for something greater.

The systems I once worked in taught me discipline, structure, and attention to detail. Today, those same lessons allow me to break down complex ideas and make them understandable for others.

That is what this series represents:

Turning complexity into clarity.

Why Artificial Intelligence Education Matters for Every Student

Why AI Literacy Is Essential for Every Student

Artificial intelligence is no longer a future concept or a specialized technology used only by experts. It is already part of everyday life for students of all ages. From smartphones and search engines to navigation apps, social media, streaming platforms, and educational tools, AI systems influence how information is accessed, decisions are made, and learning takes place.

Because AI is embedded in daily life, understanding it is no longer optional. It is a foundational skill, similar to digital literacy and critical thinking. Students do not need to become programmers or engineers, but they do need to understand what AI is, how it works at a basic level, and how it affects their lives.

AI education should not be limited to computer science classrooms. Every student interacts with AI systems daily. Teaching students how these systems function empowers them to become informed users rather than passive consumers of technology.

This book is designed to make artificial intelligence understandable, approachable, and relevant. It focuses on clarity, responsibility, and real-world understanding to help students prepare for a future where humans and intelligent systems work side by side.

IntelliGloss AI Education Series

Teaching how AI actually works—from hardware to power to global systems.

Why AI Education Matters

Artificial intelligence is already shaping how students learn, write, research, and solve problems.

Yet many students—and educators—are using AI tools without understanding how these systems actually work.

Schools need more than access to technology.
They need structured, responsible AI education.

Our Approach

The IntelliGloss AI Education Series is designed to help students move beyond simply using AI tools and begin understanding artificial intelligence as a complete system.

Students learn how AI is built, how it operates, and how it connects to the real world.

The IntelliGloss Framework

Our books introduce AI through a clear and connected system:

Chip Family — the hardware that powers AI

Watts Family — the rate at which AI uses power

Energy Family — the total power AI consumes over time

Infrastructure Family — the global systems that support AI

This framework helps students understand AI from the inside out.

Built for the Classroom

Each book includes:

Structured chapters aligned with semester learning

Clear explanations designed for student understanding

Reflection sections with learning objectives

Worksheets, quizzes, and answer keys

Teacher Implementation Guides

Supporting Schools and Educators

The IntelliGloss series supports:

Responsible and ethical AI use

Student data awareness and safety

Critical thinking and digital literacy

Classroom-ready instruction for grades 6–12 and beyond

What This Book Is—and What It Is Not

Many people today are becoming familiar with artificial intelligence through tools like ChatGPT, Microsoft Copilot, Canva, and other AI-powered applications. These tools can help with writing, answering questions, creating images, and completing everyday tasks.

In addition to these tools, you may also hear terms such as **AI agents, agentic AI, autonomous systems, and generative AI**. While these may sound complex, they are all part of the same evolving landscape of artificial intelligence technologies.

This book is not a guide on how to use those tools.

Instead, it explains what makes those tools possible.

Behind every AI tool is a system made up of multiple layers working together. At the most basic level, information is represented as bits and processed through powerful computer chips. That information is organized into data, broken into tokens, and then processed by algorithms and models that allow the system to recognize patterns, generate responses, and perform tasks.

These components—chips, bits, tokens, data, algorithms, and models—work together as a complete system. While users may only see the tool, the real intelligence comes from how these underlying parts interact behind the scenes.

Artificial intelligence can also be understood in terms of different levels of capability. Most of the AI systems used today fall under **Artificial Narrow Intelligence (ANI)**, which is designed to perform specific tasks, such as answering questions or generating content. More advanced forms, such as **Artificial General Intelligence (AGI)** and **Artificial Superintelligence (ASI)** represent future possibilities where AI could match or exceed human-level thinking. While these advanced levels are still theoretical, understanding the differences helps provide a broader view of where AI is today and where it may be heading.

For students, parents, and educators, this distinction is important. Learning how to use AI tools is helpful, but understanding how they work—and where they fit within the larger AI landscape— builds stronger thinking, better decision-making, and more responsible use.

Most importantly, artificial intelligence does not make decisions on its own. It does not take responsibility for actions or outcomes. AI systems generate responses based on data and patterns, but it is always the human who decides what to do with that information.

This book is designed to make these underlying systems clear and accessible, even for readers who are new to artificial intelligence.

Artificial intelligence is still in its early stages of development. As these technologies continue to grow, those who understand the foundation behind them will be better prepared to adapt, question, and use them wisely.

Who This Book Is For

This book is designed for educators, school leaders, and curriculum developers guiding students in an age of rapidly advancing technology.

Artificial intelligence is already influencing how students learn, research, and communicate. Yet many educators have not received formal training in how these systems work or how they should be addressed in the classroom.

This book helps bridge that gap by providing clear explanations and practical frameworks for understanding artificial intelligence in an educational setting.

How Schools Can Use This Book

This book supports schools in developing a structured approach to artificial intelligence literacy.

It can be used for:

Professional development for educators

Classroom discussions and activities

Curriculum support across subject areas

Policy and academic integrity conversations

Rather than focusing on specific tools, this book emphasizes lasting principles that help students understand, evaluate, and use AI responsibly.

Closing Perspective

Artificial intelligence will continue to evolve. With the right knowledge and leadership, schools can ensure that students not only use these technologies, but understand them, question them, and apply them responsibly.

IntelliGloss is more than a book series. It is a structured approach to preparing students for a future shaped by artificial intelligence.

Rather than focusing only on how to use AI tools, this series helps students understand how AI actually works—from its foundational building blocks to real-world applications.

"Before exploring the technical structure of artificial intelligence, it is equally important to understand the human principles that guide its use."

Human Values Family

Definition

The Human Values Family in artificial intelligence represents the guiding principles that shape how AI systems are created, used, and integrated into society. These values include ethics, responsibility, trust, and human well-being.

Artificial intelligence may be built on data, algorithms, and computational systems, but its true impact is measured by how it affects people. For this reason, AI is not only a technical system—it is a human-centered system.

Key Concepts

The Human Values Family exists to ensure that artificial intelligence serves humanity in a positive and responsible way. While AI systems can process information and generate outcomes, they do not possess judgment, empathy, or moral understanding.

This means that human values must guide every stage of AI development—from design to deployment.

AI reflects the intentions, decisions, and assumptions of the people who build and use it. If those values are not carefully considered, AI systems can unintentionally produce biased, harmful, or misleading results.

Understanding human values in AI is not optional—it is essential.

Core Elements of the Human Values Family

Ethics
Ethics in AI refers to making decisions that are fair, just, and respectful of human rights. This includes minimizing bias, protecting privacy, and ensuring transparency in how systems operate.

Responsibility
Responsibility means that humans remain accountable for AI systems. Developers, educators, organizations, and users must take ownership of how AI is used and the outcomes it produces.

Trust
Trust is critical for the successful adoption of AI. People must feel confident that AI systems are reliable, safe, and aligned with their best interests.

Human Well-Being
AI should enhance human life—not replace, harm, or diminish it. This includes supporting learning, improving access to information, and creating opportunities while maintaining human dignity.

Real-World Connection

Artificial intelligence is already influencing how people learn, communicate, and make decisions. From search engines to classroom tools, AI is shaping daily experiences.

Without clear human values guiding these systems, there is a risk of reinforcing misinformation, bias, or unrealistic expectations.

For students, this means learning not only how to use AI tools, but how to question them, evaluate their outputs, and understand their limitations.

Applications in Education

In the classroom, the Human Values Family helps students develop critical thinking and ethical awareness. Teachers can use this framework to guide discussions about fairness, responsibility, and the impact of technology on society.

Students can explore questions such as:

How should AI be used responsibly?

What makes an AI system fair?

How does technology influence human behavior?

This approach supports both technical understanding and responsible decision-making.

Benefits

Teaching human values in AI helps students:

Develop ethical awareness

Strengthen critical thinking

Understand the societal impact of technology

Become responsible users and future creators of AI

It ensures that learning about AI goes beyond functionality and includes responsibility.

Challenges

Human values are not always universal. Different cultures, communities, and individuals may have different perspectives on what is considered fair or ethical.

Additionally, AI technology is evolving rapidly, often faster than policies and guidelines can keep up. This makes it essential for educators and students to stay informed and adaptable.

Summary

The Human Values Family reminds us that artificial intelligence is not just about machines—it is about people.

By focusing on ethics, responsibility, trust, and human well-being, students can learn to use AI thoughtfully and responsibly.

Understanding these principles helps prepare learners to navigate a world where artificial intelligence plays an increasingly important role in everyday life.

Executive Summary

IntelliGloss AI Education Series

Teaching How Artificial Intelligence Actually Works

Artificial intelligence is already shaping how students learn, write, research, and make decisions. Yet in many classrooms, students are being introduced to AI tools without understanding how these systems actually function.

This creates a critical gap.

Students may become efficient users of technology, but without foundational knowledge, they are not equipped to think critically, evaluate outputs, or use AI responsibly. As AI continues to expand across every industry, this gap will only grow more significant.

The **IntelliGloss AI Education Series** was created to address this challenge.

The Problem

Most current approaches to AI in education focus on tool usage rather than system understanding. As a result:

Students rely on AI without understanding its limitations

Educators lack structured frameworks for teaching AI concepts

Key terms such as generative AI, agentic AI, and autonomy are often introduced without clear definitions

Responsibility and ethical use are not consistently emphasized

Without clarity, artificial intelligence becomes difficult to teach, difficult to learn, and difficult to manage in a school environment.

The Solution

The IntelliGloss AI Education Series provides a structured, classroom-ready approach to artificial intelligence literacy for grades 6–12.

Rather than focusing on individual tools, this series teaches students how AI works as a complete system—from foundational components to real-world applications.

Students learn to move beyond surface-level interaction and develop true understanding.

The IntelliGloss Framework

The series introduces AI through a clear and connected structure, including:

Foundational building blocks such as data, algorithms, tokens, and models

System-level understanding through categories such as intelligence level, behavior, and control

Real-world context through applications, limitations, and responsible use

Human-centered learning through ethics, responsibility, trust, and student safety

This structured approach transforms artificial intelligence from a confusing concept into an understandable system.

Instructional Design

Each book in the series is designed for practical classroom use and includes:

Structured chapters aligned with instructional pacing

Clear, student-friendly explanations

Reflection sections to reinforce understanding

Worksheets, quizzes, and answer keys

Teacher implementation support

No prior technical background is required for educators or students.

Guiding Principle

A central message of the IntelliGloss series is:

Artificial Intelligence is a tool—not a decision maker.

Students learn that while AI can support thinking and provide information, all decisions, actions, and responsibilities remain with humans. This principle reinforces critical thinking, accountability, and responsible technology use.

Why It Matters

AI literacy is no longer optional. It is a foundational skill.

Students who understand how AI works will be better prepared to:

Think critically about information

Adapt to emerging technologies

Use AI responsibly and ethically

Succeed in an increasingly AI-driven world

Our Goal

The IntelliGloss AI Education Series is designed to help schools move beyond simply using artificial intelligence tools and toward a deeper understanding of how these systems actually work.

By providing clear structure, defined concepts, and real-world context, this series equips students and educators with the knowledge needed to think critically, evaluate information, and use AI responsibly.

The goal is not just to introduce technology—but to build understanding, confidence, and accountability in an AI-driven world.

This is not just about learning to use AI—it is about preparing students to understand it, question it, and lead with it.

Clarity leads to confidence.
Understanding leads to responsible use.

Mission Statement

The mission of the IntelliGloss AI Education Series is to make artificial intelligence clear, structured, and accessible for every student and educator.

In a world where AI is rapidly transforming how information is created, used, and understood, this series is designed to move beyond surface-level interaction and provide a deeper understanding of how intelligent systems actually work.

Through clear explanations, organized frameworks, and real-world context, IntelliGloss equips learners with the ability to think critically, evaluate information, and engage with technology responsibly.

This mission is grounded in a simple belief:
students should not only learn how to use artificial intelligence—they should understand it.

By building both technical awareness and human-centered understanding, the IntelliGloss AI Education Series prepares students to navigate, question, and shape a future increasingly influenced by intelligent technologies.

The goal is not just to keep up with artificial intelligence—but to understand it, guide it, and use it responsibly.

Vision Statement

The vision of the IntelliGloss AI Education Series is to create a future where artificial intelligence is clearly understood, responsibly used, and thoughtfully integrated into education and everyday life.

In this future, students are not passive users of technology, but informed thinkers who understand how intelligent systems work, recognize their limitations, and apply them with purpose and responsibility.

Educators are equipped with clear frameworks and structured resources that make artificial intelligence accessible, teachable, and meaningful across all subjects—not just in technical fields.

Schools become environments where technology is not simply adopted, but understood—where students are encouraged to question, evaluate, and engage with AI in ways that support learning, creativity, and ethical awareness.

As artificial intelligence continues to evolve, this vision supports a generation that is prepared not only to adapt to change, but to lead it with knowledge, confidence, and integrity.

The future of artificial intelligence will not be defined by technology alone—but by the understanding and responsibility of those who use it.

Connecting AI Understanding to Cybersecurity Awareness

Definition

Understanding artificial intelligence is the first step toward understanding cybersecurity. While cybersecurity focuses on protecting systems, data, and users, artificial intelligence explains how those systems are built, how they function, and where they may be vulnerable.

The Connection

Every AI system is made up of components such as data, algorithms, models, and infrastructure. These same components are also the targets of cybersecurity threats.

When students understand:

How data is collected and stored

How algorithms make decisions

How AI models process information

How systems operate across frontend and backend layers

They begin to recognize where risks can exist and how systems can be misused.

Why This Matters

In today's digital world, students are not just users of technology—they are participants in complex systems powered by artificial intelligence.

Without understanding how these systems work:

Technology becomes something they trust without question

Risks become harder to recognize

Decisions are made without awareness of consequences

With understanding:

Students become more aware of how their data is used

They recognize how systems can be manipulated

They make more informed and responsible choices

Building Digital Readiness

Digital readiness is not only about using tools. It is about understanding the systems behind those tools.

By learning how AI works, students develop:

Awareness of digital environments

Confidence in navigating technology

A foundation for future learning, including cybersecurity

Conclusion

Cybersecurity begins with understanding.

Before students can protect systems, they must first understand how those systems are built and how they operate. This is why learning artificial intelligence is not only about innovation—it is also about responsibility.

The Foundational Families of Artificial Intelligence

Introduction

Artificial intelligence is often described as a powerful technology, but in reality, it is not a single system. It is a combination of multiple components working together to create intelligent behavior.

To better understand how artificial intelligence works, it is helpful to break it down into organized groups. In the IntelliGloss framework, these groups are called **Foundational Families of Artificial Intelligence**

Each family represents a key part of how AI systems are built and operate. Some families focus on how information is created and stored. Others focus on how machines learn, make decisions, process language, or perform tasks. Additional families represent the physical hardware, energy systems, and global infrastructure that make artificial intelligence possible.

When these families work together, they form a complete AI system.

This approach allows students and educators to move beyond simply using artificial intelligence tools and begin to understand what is happening behind the scenes. Instead of viewing AI as a mystery, learners can see it as a structured system made up of clearly defined components.

The diagram on the next page provides a visual overview of these families and how they connect to form the foundation of artificial intelligence.

By learning each family step by step, students develop a deeper understanding of how AI systems process information, learn from data, and interact with the world.

Understanding the Foundational Families of Artificial Intelligence is the first step toward true AI literacy.

The Foundational Families of Artificial Intelligence

The Foundational Families of Artificial Intelligence

Family	Role	Description
Bit Family	Digital Building Blocks	The smallest unit of digital information (0 or 1). All computing systems begin with bits.
Algorithm Family	Reasoning Engine	Step-by-step instructions that tell computers how to solve problems and process information.
Token Family	Language Units	Pieces of text used by AI models to understand and generate human language.
Parameter Family	Learning Adjustment System	Adjustable numerical values inside AI models that allow them to learn patterns from data.
Data Family	Learning Material	The information AI studies in order to learn patterns, relationships, and knowledge.

Family	Role	Description
Logic Family	Decision Rules	The reasoning structures that allow AI systems to make decisions and evaluate conditions.
Memory Family	Information Storage	Systems that store and retrieve information so AI models can access past knowledge and context.
Knowledge Family	Understanding & Meaning	Structured information that allows AI to represent facts, relationships, and concepts.
Neural Network Family	Learning Brain	Interconnected layers of artificial neurons that enable AI systems to recognize patterns, learn from data, and make predictions.
AI Model Family	Intelligence Engine	The trained system that uses data, parameters, and neural networks to perform tasks such as prediction, classification, and generation.
AI Translator Architecture Family	Language Conversion System	Systems that transform input into output, enabling AI to convert text, speech, or images into meaningful responses.
AI Agent Family	Action and Task Execution System	AI systems designed to perceive information, make decisions, and carry out tasks autonomously or semi-autonomously.
Chip Family	Hardware Brain	Physical processors (GPUs, TPUs, CPUs, NPUs) that perform AI computations.
Watts Family	Energy Power	The electrical power required to run AI hardware and data centers.
AI Energy Family	Energy Source System	The total energy consumed over time to operate AI systems, including training and real-time usage.
Infrastructure Family	Global Support System	Data centers, internet networks, cloud systems, and global infrastructure that allow AI to operate and scale.
Ingredient Family	System Composition	The essential components that come together to create an AI system, including data, algorithms, models, hardware, and energy.
Qubit Family	Quantum Information Units	Quantum bits that can represent multiple states simultaneously, forming the foundation of quantum computing.

To begin understanding how artificial intelligence is built, we start with the most fundamental unit of all computing systems: the bit.

The Bit Family

Introduction

The Bit Family represents the starting point of all digital technology. Every computer system, application, and artificial intelligence model is built from bits—the smallest unit of information in computing.

A bit can hold one of two values: 0 or 1. While this may seem simple, these two values form the foundation of everything digital. When bits are combined and organized, they create larger units of data that allow computers to store text, display images, play videos, and run complex systems.

From a single bit to massive data systems, all digital information follows this same structure. This is how computers are able to represent and process the world in a form they can understand.

In artificial intelligence, bits are essential because they store the data that models learn from, process the calculations that drive decision-making, and support the systems that generate responses.

Understanding the Bit Family helps students see how simple binary signals grow into powerful technologies. It reveals that behind every advanced AI system is a foundation built from the most basic building blocks of information.

Bit Family — Visual Understanding of Data Size

How Much Data Can Each Unit Hold? (Simple Examples)

Unit	Size	Photos (Approx.)	Video (Approx. Hours)
Bit	1 bit	N/A	N/A
Byte	8 bits	1 character	N/A
Kilobyte (KB)	~1,000 bytes	Part of a paragraph	N/A
Megabyte (MB)	~1,000 KB	~1 photo	~1 minute of video
Gigabyte (GB)	~1,000 MB	~250 photos	~1–2 hours of video
Terabyte (TB)	~1,000 GB	~250,000 photos	~1,000–2,000 hours of video
Petabyte (PB)	~1,000 TB	~250 million photos	~1–2 million hours of video
Exabyte (EB)	~1,000 PB	~250 billion photos	~1–2 billion hours of video
Zettabyte (ZB)	~1,000 EB	~250 trillion photos	~1–2 trillion hours of video
Yottabyte (YB)	~1,000 ZB	~250 quadrillion photos	~1–2 quadrillion hours of video

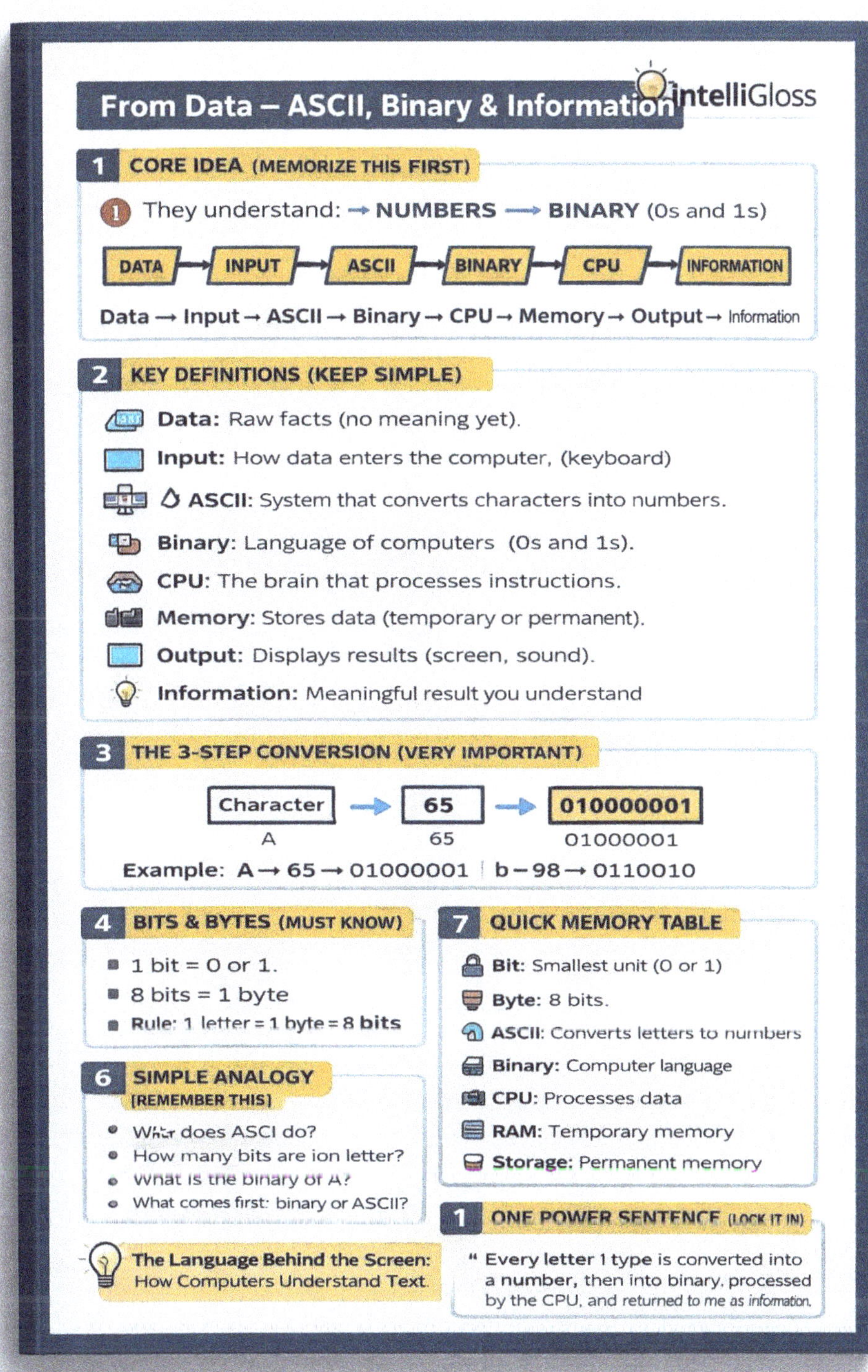

⚙ *The Algorithm Family*

Definition and Overview

The **Algorithm Family** represents the *thinking engine* of artificial intelligence — the set of mathematical instructions that guide how AI analyzes data, learns patterns, and makes decisions.

An **algorithm** is a sequence of steps designed to solve a problem or complete a task. In AI, algorithms tell the system *how to learn*, *how to predict*, and *how to improve* with every iteration.

In simple terms:

The Algorithm Family is the *logic of intelligence* — the invisible code that transforms data into decisions and predictions into progress.

🔴 How Algorithms Power AI

Every AI system — from simple chatbots to large-scale deep learning models — relies on algorithms as its foundation.
They determine how the model:

Processes and cleans data,

Identifies relationships between variables,

Learns from feedback, and

Improves over time.

Without algorithms, even the most powerful dataset or neural network would remain static and lifeless.

In essence, **algorithms are the teachers** that train AI how to think.

⚙️ *Why the Algorithm Family Matters*

Algorithms are what separate automation from intelligence.
They allow machines to **reason**, **adapt**, and **learn** — not just follow commands.
For prompt engineers, understanding algorithmic behavior helps explain *why* AI sometimes misunderstands a question, repeats patterns, or changes tone after feedback.

Every AI response you receive follows an underlying process — a pattern recognition journey from input to output.

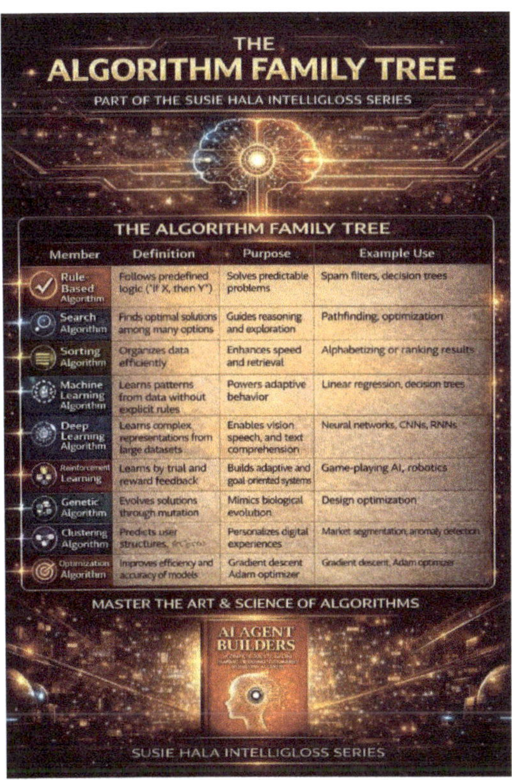

Member	Definition	Purpose	Example Use
Rule-Based Algorithm	Follows predefined logic ("If X, then Y")	Solves predictable problems	Spam filters, decision trees
Search Algorithm	Finds optimal solutions among many options	Guides reasoning and exploration	Pathfinding, optimization
Sorting Algorithm	Organizes data efficiently	Enhances speed and retrieval	Alphabetizing or ranking results
Machine Learning Algorithm	Learns patterns from data without explicit rules	Powers adaptive behavior	Linear regression, decision trees
Deep Learning Algorithm	Learns complex representations from large datasets	Enables vision, speech, and text comprehension	Neural networks, CNNs, RNNs
Reinforcement Learning	Learns by trial and reward feedback	Builds adaptive and goal-oriented systems	Game-playing AI, robotics
Genetic Algorithm	Evolves solutions through mutation	Mimics biological evolution	Design optimization
Clustering Algorithm	Predicts user structures, groups	Personalizes digital experiences	Market segmentation, anomaly detection
Optimization Algorithm	Improves efficiency and accuracy of models	Gradient descent, Adam optimizer	Gradient descent, Adam optimizer

🌐 Analogy for Everyday Readers

Imagine AI as a chef in a kitchen:

> The **Dataset Family** provides the ingredients.

> The **Knowledge Family** gives the recipes.

> The **Algorithm Family** is the *cooking process* — mixing, heating, tasting, and adjusting until the dish is perfect.

Just as cooking methods determine the quality of food, algorithms determine the quality of intelligence.

⚡ Algorithm Efficiency and Energy Use

Not all algorithms are equal.
Some are **fast but shallow**, while others are **deep but energy-intensive**.
Training large AI models requires algorithms that can handle billions of calculations per second — powered by the **Watts Family** (energy) and executed through the **Chip Family** (hardware).

The design of efficient algorithms directly affects sustainability in AI — minimizing power consumption while maximizing accuracy and speed.

�֎ Algorithms and Prompt Engineering

For prompt engineers, algorithms explain *how* the AI arrives at its answers.
When a model gives inconsistent or off-topic results, it's often due to:

Misinterpretation of input signals (input encoding),

Bias in training algorithms, or

Overfitting to certain data patterns.

Knowing this helps you craft prompts that guide the AI's decision-making — not just its output.

💬 Quick Takeaway: The Algorithm Family is the reasoning heart of AI.
It transforms information into understanding and enables machines to think, learn, and evolve like digital problem-solvers.

Absolutely, partner — this is a powerful section in your book because **tokens are where AI meets language**. I'll keep this aligned with your style: clear, structured, and school-district ready.

Token Family Introduction

The Token Family represents one of the most important bridges between human language and artificial intelligence. While humans communicate using words, sentences, and meaning, AI systems do not understand language in the same way. Instead, they rely on tokens—small units of text that allow machines to process, analyze, and generate language step by step.

A token can be a word, part of a word, a character, or even punctuation. When a student types a sentence into an AI system, that sentence is not read as a whole idea. It is first broken down into tokens. These tokens become the input that the AI model uses to recognize patterns, predict outcomes, and generate responses.

The Token Family works closely with several other foundational families in artificial intelligence. It connects directly with the Data Family, which provides the text used for training, and the Neural Network Family, which processes token patterns to produce intelligent outputs. It also plays a key role in the AI Translator Architecture Family, where tokens are transformed, analyzed, and reassembled into meaningful responses.

Understanding tokens helps students see what is happening behind the scenes when they interact with AI tools. Instead of viewing AI as a "magic system," they begin to understand that every response is built from sequences of tokens processed through mathematical models.

In simple terms, if language is what humans speak, tokens are what AI understands.

Token Family Breakdown Chart

Component	Role	Description	Example
Tokenization	Input Conversion	The process of breaking text into smaller units (tokens) that AI can process	"Artificial Intelligence" → "Artificial" + "Intelligence"
Tokens	Language Units	The individual pieces of text used by AI models for understanding and generation	"AI", "learn", "ing", "."
Subword Tokens	Efficiency Units	Words split into smaller parts to handle unknown or complex vocabulary	"unbelievable" → "un", "believ", "able"
Character Tokens	Fine-Grained Units	Text broken down into individual characters for detailed processing	"AI" → "A" + "I"
Vocabulary (Token Set)	Token Library	The complete set of tokens an AI model recognizes and uses	GPT models have thousands to millions of tokens
Encoding	Token Mapping	Converting tokens into numerical representations for computation	"AI" → [1234, 5678] (example IDs)
Decoding	Output Reconstruction	Converting numerical outputs back into readable text	[1234, 5678] → "AI system"
Context Window	Memory Limit	The number of tokens an AI can process at one time	Example: 8,000 tokens ≈ several pages of text
Token Embeddings	Meaning Representation	Mathematical vectors that capture relationships between tokens	"king" and "queen" have similar embeddings
Token Prediction	Language Generation	The process of predicting the next token in a sequence	"AI is" → predicts "powerful"

The Token Family reminds us that behind every intelligent response is a structured sequence of tokens working together. What feels like natural conversation to humans is, for AI, a carefully processed stream of language units transformed into meaning.

Parameter Family Introduction

The Parameter Family represents the internal learning system of artificial intelligence. While tokens provide the language and data provides the learning material, parameters are what allow AI systems to adjust, improve, and make intelligent decisions over time.

In simple terms, parameters are numerical values inside an AI model that change as the system learns. These values are not visible to users, but they play a critical role in how the model understands patterns, relationships, and meaning. Every time an AI system is trained, it adjusts its parameters to better predict outcomes and generate accurate responses.

Parameters exist throughout neural networks, where they act as the connections between artificial neurons. Each connection has a weight, which determines how important a particular piece of information is. During training, these weights are continuously adjusted based on data, allowing the system to improve its performance.

The Parameter Family works closely with the Data Family, which provides the information needed for learning, and the Neural Network Family, which organizes how parameters are structured and applied. It also supports the Token Family by helping the model interpret and predict sequences of language.

Understanding parameters helps students recognize that AI is not simply programmed with fixed rules. Instead, it learns by adjusting internal values that guide how it processes information. These adjustments are what allow AI systems to evolve from simple pattern recognition to complex reasoning and decision-making.

In essence, if data is what AI learns from, parameters are how AI learns.

Parameter Family Breakdown Chart

Component	Role	Description	Example
Parameters	Learning Values	Numerical values inside an AI model that are adjusted during training	Millions or billions of values inside a model
Weights	Connection Strength	Values that determine how strongly one neuron influences another	A higher weight = stronger influence
Bias	Adjustment Factor	A value added to help the model shift and fine-tune outputs	Helps improve accuracy in predictions
Training Process	Learning Mechanism	The process of adjusting parameters using data to improve performance	Model improves after analyzing many examples
Loss Function	Error Measurement	Measures how far the model's prediction is from the correct answer	Lower loss = better performance
Optimization Algorithm	Adjustment Strategy	Method used to update parameters efficiently	Gradient Descent adjusts weights step by step
Gradient	Direction of Change	Indicates how parameters should change to reduce error	Shows whether to increase or decrease a value
Backpropagation	Learning Process	System that sends error signals backward to update parameters	Adjusts earlier layers based on output error

Component	Role	Description	Example
Hyperparameters	Control Settings	External settings that guide how training happens (not learned)	Learning rate, batch size
Model Size	Capacity Indicator	The total number of parameters in a model	Larger models = more learning capacity

The Parameter Family is the hidden engine of learning in artificial intelligence. While users interact with outputs, it is the continuous adjustment of parameters behind the scenes that makes intelligent behavior possible.

Data Family Introduction

The Data Family represents the foundation of learning in artificial intelligence. Every AI system depends on data to develop knowledge, recognize patterns, and make decisions. Without data, artificial intelligence cannot learn, adapt, or function effectively.

Data can take many forms, including text, images, audio, video, and numerical information. These inputs provide the raw material that AI systems analyze during training. By studying large amounts of data, AI models begin to identify patterns, relationships, and structures that allow them to make predictions and generate responses.

The quality and diversity of data play a critical role in how well an AI system performs. Accurate, balanced, and relevant data helps models produce reliable results, while poor or biased data can lead to incorrect or unfair outcomes. This is why data collection, preparation, and evaluation are essential steps in the development of responsible AI systems.

The Data Family works closely with the Parameter Family, which adjusts internal values based on data, and the Neural Network Family, which processes and organizes data through layers of computation. It also supports the Token Family when dealing with language, as text data is converted into tokens for analysis.

Understanding the Data Family helps students recognize that AI does not "know" things on its own. Instead, it learns from the information it is given. The more meaningful and well-prepared the data, the more capable the AI system becomes.

In simple terms, data is the source of knowledge, and it is the starting point for all artificial intelligence.

Data Family Breakdown Chart

Component	Role	Description	Example
Data	Learning Material	Raw information used by AI systems to learn patterns and relationships	Text, images, audio, numbers
Dataset	Organized Collection	A structured group of data used for training and evaluation	A folder of labeled images
Training Data	Learning Input	Data used to teach the AI model during training	Thousands of sentences for a language model
Validation Data	Performance Check	Data used to tune the model during training without directly learning from it	Helps prevent overfitting
Test Data	Final Evaluation	Data used to measure how well the model performs after training	New unseen examples
Structured Data	Organized Format	Data arranged in tables with clear categories	Spreadsheets, databases
Unstructured Data	Flexible Format	Data without a predefined structure	Text documents, images, videos
Labeled Data	Guided Learning	Data tagged with correct answers to guide training	Image labeled "cat" or "dog"
Unlabeled Data	Self-Learning Input	Data without labels, used in unsupervised learning	Raw text without categories
Data Quality	Accuracy Measure	The reliability and correctness of data	Clean, complete, and consistent data
Data Bias	Imbalance Issue	When data does not represent all groups fairly	Skewed or incomplete datasets
Data Preprocessing	Preparation Step	Cleaning and organizing data before training	Removing errors, formatting text

The Data Family reminds us that artificial intelligence is only as strong as the information it learns from. High-quality data leads to meaningful insights, while poor data can limit or misguide intelligent systems.

Memory Family Introduction

The Memory Family represents how artificial intelligence systems store, retain, and retrieve information. Just as humans rely on memory to recall past experiences, learn new concepts, and make decisions, AI systems depend on memory to access previously processed information and maintain context.

In artificial intelligence, memory is not a single component but a collection of mechanisms that allow systems to handle information over time. Some forms of memory are short-term, holding information temporarily while a task is being completed. Other forms are long-term, storing learned knowledge that can be used across different tasks and interactions.

Memory plays a critical role in enabling AI systems to understand sequences, maintain context in conversations, and improve decision-making. For example, when a user interacts with a language model, the system uses memory to keep track of previous words, sentences, or prompts in order to generate coherent and relevant responses.

The Memory Family works closely with the Data Family, which provides the information to be stored, and the Parameter Family, which encodes learned knowledge within the model. It also supports the Neural Network Family by enabling systems to process sequences and retain important patterns over time.

Understanding the Memory Family helps students see that AI is not simply reacting to individual inputs in isolation. Instead, it relies on stored information and contextual awareness to produce meaningful and consistent outputs.

In simple terms, if data is what AI learns from, memory is how AI remembers and uses what it has learned.

Memory Family Breakdown Chart

Component	Role	Description	Example
Memory	Information Storage	The ability of an AI system to store and access information	Retaining previous inputs in a task
Short-Term Memory	Temporary Storage	Holds information for immediate processing	Keeping track of words in a sentence
Long-Term Memory	Persistent Storage	Stores learned knowledge for future use	Knowledge embedded in model parameters
Context Memory	Conversation Tracking	Maintains information within a specific interaction	Remembering earlier parts of a prompt
Working Memory	Active Processing	Handles information currently being used in computation	Processing a sequence step by step
External Memory	Extended Storage	Memory stored outside the model for retrieval	Databases, vector stores
Internal Memory	Embedded Knowledge	Information stored within the model itself	Learned patterns inside neural networks
Sequence Memory	Order Awareness	Tracks the order of inputs over time	Understanding sentence structure
Retrieval Mechanism	Access System	Retrieves stored information when needed	Searching relevant past data

Component	Role	Description	Example
Attention Mechanism	Focus System	Highlights important parts of memory for processing	Focusing on key words in a sentence
Memory Capacity	Storage Limit	The amount of information the system can handle at once	Context window size

The Memory Family shows that intelligence is not just about processing information in the moment, but about retaining, organizing, and using knowledge over time to create meaningful understanding.

Knowledge Family Introduction

The Knowledge Family represents how artificial intelligence organizes, connects, and uses information to create understanding. While data provides raw information and memory stores it, knowledge is what gives that information meaning and structure.

In artificial intelligence, knowledge is not simply a collection of facts. It is the result of identifying relationships, patterns, and connections within data. AI systems use knowledge to recognize concepts, make decisions, and generate meaningful responses. This allows machines to move beyond simple data processing and toward more intelligent behavior.

Knowledge can be represented in different ways within AI systems. Some forms are structured, such as databases and knowledge graphs, where relationships between concepts are clearly defined. Other forms are learned implicitly through neural networks, where patterns are encoded within parameters and used to guide predictions.

The Knowledge Family works closely with the Data Family, which provides the information needed to build knowledge, and the Memory Family, which stores and retrieves that information. It also connects with the Parameter Family, where learned knowledge is embedded within the model, and the Neural Network Family, which processes and organizes that knowledge.

Understanding the Knowledge Family helps students recognize that AI systems do not simply memorize information. Instead, they learn how pieces of information relate to one another, allowing them to interpret meaning, solve problems, and respond intelligently.

In simple terms, if data is information and memory stores it, knowledge is the understanding that makes it useful.

Knowledge Family Breakdown Chart

Component	Role	Description	Example
Knowledge	Understanding System	Organized information that allows AI to interpret meaning and make decisions	Recognizing relationships between concepts
Facts	Basic Information	Individual pieces of information stored within a system	"Water freezes at 0°C"
Relationships	Connection Mapping	Links between pieces of information that create meaning	"Teacher teaches student"
Knowledge Representation	Structure System	Methods used to organize and store knowledge in AI	Knowledge graphs, semantic networks
Knowledge Graph	Network Mapping	A structured representation of entities and their relationships	Google Knowledge Graph
Semantic Understanding	Meaning Interpretation	The ability to understand meaning behind words and data	Understanding synonyms and context
Inference	Reasoning Process	Drawing conclusions based on known information	If A = B and B = C, then A = C
Rules	Decision Framework	Logical guidelines used to make decisions	If temperature < 0°C → freeze
Ontology	Concept Framework	A structured system defining categories and relationships	Classification of animals
Explicit Knowledge	Direct Information	Clearly defined and stored knowledge	Rules, databases
Implicit Knowledge	Learned Patterns	Knowledge learned through experience and data	Patterns learned by neural networks
Knowledge Integration	System Coordination	Combining information from multiple sources	Merging text, images, and data

The Knowledge Family transforms information into understanding, allowing artificial intelligence to move beyond data and memory into meaningful reasoning and intelligent decision-making.

AI Model Family Introduction

The AI Model Family represents the core system within artificial intelligence that performs tasks such as prediction, classification, and content generation. It is the part of AI that users interact with, whether they are asking questions, generating images, or analyzing data.

An AI model is a trained system that has learned patterns from data. During training, the model processes large amounts of information and adjusts its internal parameters to improve accuracy.

Once trained, the model can take new input and produce meaningful output based on what it has learned.

AI models can take many forms depending on their purpose. Some models are designed to recognize images, others to understand language, and others to make decisions or predictions. Large Language Models (LLMs), for example, are designed to process and generate human language by predicting sequences of tokens.

The AI Model Family works closely with the Data Family, which provides the learning material, and the Parameter Family, which stores learned patterns. It also relies on the Neural Network Family for structure and the Chip and Infrastructure Families for execution and deployment.

Understanding the AI Model Family helps students see that AI is not just a concept, but a working system that has been trained to perform specific tasks. It is the engine that transforms input into output.

In simple terms, if AI is the system, the model is the part that actually does the thinking and producing.

AI Model Family Breakdown Chart

Component	Role	Description	Example
AI Model	Core System	The trained system that performs tasks	Chatbot, image generator
Training	Learning Process	Process of teaching the model using data	Learning from datasets
Inference	Output Generation	Using the trained model to produce results	Answering a question
Model Architecture	Structural Design	Defines how the model is built	Neural networks, transformers
Parameters	Learned Values	Internal values adjusted during training	Billions of weights
Input Data	Entry Information	Data provided to the model for processing	User prompt
Output Data	Result	The response or prediction generated	AI-generated text
Model Types	Functional Categories	Different kinds of models for different tasks	Classification, generation
Fine-Tuning	Model Adjustment	Improving a model for specific tasks	Custom-trained AI
Pretrained Model	Base System	A model trained on large datasets before use	General-purpose AI

Component	Role	Description	Example
Evaluation	Performance Check	Measuring how well the model performs	Accuracy, loss metrics

The AI Model Family represents the working core of artificial intelligence, where learned patterns are transformed into meaningful actions, predictions, and responses.

Neural Network Family Introduction

The Neural Network Family represents the structural foundation of how artificial intelligence learns and processes information. Inspired by the human brain, neural networks are systems of interconnected units, often called neurons, that work together to analyze data, recognize patterns, and make decisions.

In artificial intelligence, a neural network is made up of layers. The input layer receives data, the hidden layers process that data, and the output layer produces a result. As information flows through these layers, the network applies mathematical transformations that allow it to detect patterns and relationships within the data.

Neural networks rely heavily on the Parameter Family, where weights and biases determine how strongly information flows between neurons. During training, these parameters are adjusted to improve the network's performance. The more the network learns, the better it becomes at recognizing patterns and making accurate predictions.

The Neural Network Family works closely with the Data Family, which provides the information needed for learning, and the Memory and Knowledge Families, which help store and organize learned information. It also supports the Token Family when processing language, allowing AI systems to interpret sequences of tokens in meaningful ways.

Understanding neural networks helps students see that AI is not simply following instructions. Instead, it is learning from examples and improving over time through layered processing and pattern recognition.

In simple terms, neural networks are the systems that allow AI to think, learn, and make sense of information.

Neural Network Family Breakdown Chart

Component	Role	Description	Example
Neural Network	Learning Structure	A system of interconnected neurons that processes data and learns patterns	Image recognition system

Component	Role	Description	Example
Neuron (Node)	Processing Unit	A basic unit that receives input, processes it, and passes output forward	A single calculation point
Input Layer	Data Entry Point	The first layer that receives raw data	Pixels of an image
Hidden Layers	Processing Layers	Intermediate layers that transform data and detect patterns	Feature detection layers
Output Layer	Result Generator	The final layer that produces predictions or decisions	"Cat" vs "Dog" classification
Weights	Signal Strength	Values that determine how strongly inputs influence outputs	Higher weight = stronger impact
Bias	Adjustment Value	Helps shift outputs to improve learning accuracy	Fine-tuning predictions
Activation Function	Decision Function	Determines whether a neuron should activate based on input	ReLU, Sigmoid
Forward Propagation	Data Flow	The process of passing input data through the network to produce output	Input → Hidden → Output
Backpropagation	Learning Process	Adjusts weights and biases based on error to improve performance	Correcting mistakes
Loss Function	Error Measurement	Calculates how far the output is from the correct answer	Prediction vs actual
Deep Neural Network	Advanced Structure	A network with many hidden layers for complex learning	Deep learning models

The Neural Network Family provides the structure that allows artificial intelligence to transform data into understanding, making it possible for machines to learn from experience and improve over time.

AI Translator Architecture Family Introduction

The AI Translator Architecture Family represents the system that transforms input into meaningful output in artificial intelligence. It acts as the bridge between what humans provide and what AI produces. Whether a user types a question, uploads an image, or speaks a command, this architecture is responsible for interpreting that input and generating a response.

In artificial intelligence, translation does not only mean converting one language to another. It refers to the broader process of transforming one form of information into another. For example, text can be translated into a response, speech can be converted into text, and images can be interpreted into descriptions. This transformation process is at the core of how modern AI systems function.

The AI Translator Architecture is built on multiple foundational families. It relies on the Token Family to break input into manageable units, the Neural Network Family to process patterns, and the Parameter Family to guide learning. It also uses knowledge and memory to maintain context and produce coherent results.

At the center of this architecture is the ability to encode and decode information. Encoding transforms input into a format the model can understand, while decoding converts processed information back into human-readable output. This continuous transformation allows AI systems to interact with users in a natural and meaningful way.

Understanding the AI Translator Architecture Family helps students see that AI is not simply responding randomly. Instead, it is systematically translating input into output through structured processes and learned patterns.

In simple terms, if tokens are the language pieces and neural networks are the brain, the AI Translator Architecture is the system that turns understanding into communication.

AI Translator Architecture Family Breakdown Chart

Component	Role	Description	Example
AI Translator Architecture	Transformation System	Converts input into meaningful output	Question → Answer
Input Processing	Data Intake	Receives and prepares user input for analysis	Text prompt entered by a user
Encoding	Input Conversion	Transforms input into numerical representations	Words → token IDs
Context Building	Meaning Formation	Organizes input into a structured understanding	Sentence context tracking
Sequence Processing	Order Handling	Maintains the correct order of information	Word sequence in a sentence
Attention Mechanism	Focus System	Identifies important parts of input data	Highlighting key words
Representation Layer	Feature Mapping	Converts data into internal representations for processing	Embeddings
Decoding	Output Generation	Converts processed data back into human-readable form	Token IDs → words
Output Generation	Response Creation	Produces the final answer or result	AI-generated response

Component	Role	Description	Example
Multimodal Translation	Cross-Format Processing	Translates between different types of data	Image → text description
Feedback Loop	Improvement Cycle	Uses results to refine future outputs	Model learning over time

The AI Translator Architecture Family shows that artificial intelligence is not just about understanding information, but about transforming it into meaningful communication that humans can use and interact with.

AI Architecture Family Introduction

The AI Architecture Family represents the overall design and structure of an artificial intelligence system. While individual families such as Data, Parameters, and Neural Networks explain how AI learns and processes information, the AI Architecture Family shows how all these components are organized and work together as a complete system.

In artificial intelligence, architecture refers to the blueprint that defines how data flows through a system, how components interact, and how decisions are produced. It determines how input is received, how it is processed, and how output is generated. A well-designed architecture allows AI systems to operate efficiently, scale to large problems, and produce reliable results.

AI architectures can vary depending on the type of system being built. Some are designed for image recognition, others for language processing, and others for decision-making or automation. Despite these differences, most architectures share common elements such as input layers, processing layers, memory components, and output mechanisms.

The AI Architecture Family connects all foundational families. It integrates the Data Family for input, the Token Family for language processing, the Neural Network Family for computation, the Parameter Family for learning, and the Memory and Knowledge Families for storing and organizing information. It also works closely with the AI Translator Architecture Family to transform input into meaningful output.

Understanding the AI Architecture Family helps students see the "big picture" of artificial intelligence. Instead of viewing AI as separate parts, they begin to understand it as a coordinated system where each component plays a specific role.

In simple terms, if individual families are the parts of AI, the AI Architecture Family is the blueprint that brings everything together into one working system.

AI Architecture Family Breakdown Chart

Component	Role	Description	Example
AI Architecture	System Blueprint	The overall design that defines how an AI system is structured and operates	ChatGPT system design
Input Layer	Data Entry Point	Receives raw input from users or external sources	Text prompt, image upload
Preprocessing Layer	Data Preparation	Cleans and organizes input data before processing	Tokenization, normalization
Processing Core	Computation Engine	The main system where data is analyzed and transformed	Neural networks, transformers
Parameter System	Learning Core	Stores adjustable values that guide learning and predictions	Model weights and biases
Memory System	Context Storage	Maintains and retrieves information during processing	Context window, external memory
Knowledge System	Understanding Layer	Organizes relationships and meaning within the system	Knowledge graphs, learned patterns
Decision Layer	Output Logic	Determines the final output based on processed data	Selecting the best response
Output Layer	Result Delivery	Presents results to the user in a usable format	Text, image, or audio response
Feedback Loop	Improvement System	Uses outcomes to refine future performance	Model updates and retraining
Scalability System	Expansion Capability	Allows the system to handle increasing data and complexity	Cloud-based AI systems
Integration Layer	System Connection	Connects AI with external tools and platforms	APIs, databases, applications

The AI Architecture Family reveals that artificial intelligence is not a single technology, but a coordinated system of interconnected components working together to transform data into intelligent outcomes.

Chip Family Introduction

The Chip Family represents the physical hardware that powers artificial intelligence systems. While software components such as data, algorithms, and neural networks define how AI works, none of these systems can function without the computing chips that perform the actual calculations.

Chips are specialized electronic components designed to process information at extremely high speeds. In artificial intelligence, these chips handle the complex mathematical operations required for training models and generating outputs. Every prediction, calculation, and response produced by an AI system is executed by hardware within the Chip Family.

Different types of chips are used depending on the needs of the system. Central Processing Units (CPUs) handle general-purpose tasks, while Graphics Processing Units (GPUs) are optimized for parallel processing, making them ideal for training neural networks. More specialized chips, such as Tensor Processing Units (TPUs) and Neural Processing Units (NPUs), are designed specifically for AI workloads, enabling faster and more efficient computation.

The Chip Family works closely with the Neural Network Family, which defines the structure of computation, and the Parameter Family, which stores the values being processed. It also connects to the Infrastructure Family, where large-scale systems of chips are organized in data centers and cloud environments.

Understanding the Chip Family helps students recognize that artificial intelligence is not purely abstract. It depends on physical machines that require power, resources, and engineering to operate. These chips are the engines that bring AI models to life.

In simple terms, if AI is the intelligence, chips are the machines that make that intelligence possible.

Chip Family Breakdown Chart

Component	Role	Description	Example
Chip (Processor)	Computation Engine	Electronic hardware that performs calculations required for AI	CPU, GPU
CPU (Central Processing Unit)	General Processor	Handles a wide range of computing tasks	Running basic applications
GPU (Graphics Processing Unit)	Parallel Processor	Processes many calculations at once, ideal for AI training	Training neural networks
TPU (Tensor Processing Unit)	AI Accelerator	Specialized chip designed for machine learning tasks	Google TPU
NPU (Neural Processing Unit)	Edge AI Processor	Optimized for running AI on devices like phones	Smartphone AI features
AI Accelerator	Performance Booster	Hardware designed to speed up AI computations	Dedicated AI chips
Memory (Hardware)	Data Storage	Stores data and instructions for processing	RAM, VRAM
Parallel Processing	Speed Mechanism	Ability to perform multiple calculations simultaneously	GPUs processing thousands of operations

Component	Role	Description	Example
Throughput	Processing Capacity	Amount of data processed over time	High-performance computing systems
Latency	Response Time	Time it takes to process a request	Faster chips = lower latency
Power Consumption	Energy Usage	Amount of energy required to run the chip	High-performance GPUs use more power
Edge Devices	Local Processing	Devices that run AI locally without cloud support	Phones, smart cameras

The Chip Family reminds us that behind every intelligent system is powerful hardware performing millions or billions of calculations, turning abstract models into real-world functionality.

Watts Family Introduction

The Watts Family represents the measurement of power used by artificial intelligence systems. While the Chip Family provides the hardware that performs computations, the Watts Family explains how much energy those systems consume while operating.

A watt is a unit of power that measures the rate at which energy is used. In artificial intelligence, watts help us understand how much electricity is required to run processors, train models, and generate responses. Every time an AI system processes data, performs calculations, or produces output, it consumes power.

Different AI systems require different levels of power depending on their size and complexity. Small systems, such as those running on mobile devices, use relatively low amounts of power. In contrast, large-scale AI models operating in data centers can require significant amounts of electricity, especially during training, where billions of calculations are performed continuously.

The Watts Family works closely with the Chip Family, which determines how efficiently computations are performed, and the Infrastructure Family, where large networks of machines operate together. It also connects to the overall design of AI systems, as more efficient models can reduce power consumption while maintaining performance.

Understanding the Watts Family helps students recognize that artificial intelligence is not only about intelligence and computation, but also about energy use and resource management. As AI continues to grow, managing power efficiently becomes an important part of building responsible and sustainable systems.

In simple terms, if chips perform the work, watts measure how much power it takes to do that work.

Watts Family Breakdown Chart

Component	Role	Description	Example
Watt (W)	Power Measurement	Unit that measures the rate of energy use	A device using 100 watts
Power Consumption	Energy Usage Rate	Amount of power used during operation	AI model running on GPUs
Energy Efficiency	Performance Balance	How effectively a system uses power to perform tasks	More output with less power
High-Performance Computing	Intensive Power Use	Systems that require large amounts of power for complex tasks	AI training clusters
Idle Power	Standby Usage	Power consumed when systems are not actively processing	Servers waiting for requests
Peak Power	Maximum Usage	Highest level of power used during heavy workloads	Training large AI models
Thermal Output	Heat Generation	Heat produced as a result of power usage	Cooling systems in data centers
Cooling Systems	Temperature Control	Systems used to manage heat from high power usage	Air or liquid cooling
Power Supply	Energy Source	Provides electricity to AI systems	Electrical grid, batteries
Edge Power Usage	Local Energy Use	Power consumption on smaller devices	Smartphones, IoT devices
Data Center Power	Large-Scale Usage	Power required for large AI operations	Server farms running AI models
Sustainable Energy	Efficiency Goal	Use of renewable energy to reduce environmental impact	Solar-powered data centers

The Watts Family highlights that intelligence comes with a cost—every AI system requires power, and understanding that power is essential for building efficient and sustainable technologies.

 Watts Family (AI Power Usage Scale)

Definition

The **Watts Family** represents the real-time power usage of artificial intelligence systems, measured in watts (W). It shows how much power AI systems consume at a given moment as they process data and perform computations.

Watts Scale

1 Watt
10 Watts
100 Watts
500 Watts
1,000 Watts (1 Kilowatt)
10,000 Watts (10 Kilowatts)
100,000 Watts (100 Kilowatts)
1,000,000 Watts (1 Megawatt)
10,000,000 Watts (10 Megawatts)
100,000,000+ Watts (100+ Megawatts)

Key Characteristics

Measured in real-world electrical power

Higher watt values indicate higher processing demand

Used to represent the scale of AI systems from small devices to large infrastructures

Closely connected to the Chip Family, Energy Family, and Infrastructure Family

Examples

Low watts → small devices and basic AI functions

Medium watts → computers and advanced applications

High watts → data centers and large AI systems

Summary

The **Watts Family** provides a numerical representation of how much power artificial intelligence systems use in real time, helping to illustrate the scale and intensity of AI operations.

🪨 Student Insight

Watts show how much power AI is using right now.

AI Energy Family Introduction

The AI Energy Family represents the total amount of energy consumed by artificial intelligence systems over time. While the Watts Family measures the rate at which power is used at any given moment, the Energy Family focuses on the accumulated energy required to perform tasks, run systems, and sustain operations.

In artificial intelligence, energy is used every time a model is trained, a system processes data, or a response is generated. Large-scale AI systems, especially those operating in data centers, can consume significant amounts of energy due to the continuous processing of massive datasets and complex computations.

Energy is typically measured over time using units such as kilowatt-hours (kWh), which reflect how much power has been used during a specific period. For example, running a high-performance AI system for several hours or days results in a total energy cost that goes beyond the moment-to-moment power usage measured in watts.

The AI Energy Family works closely with the Watts Family, which provides the rate of power consumption, and the Chip Family, which determines how efficiently computations are performed. It also connects to the Infrastructure Family, where large-scale systems operate continuously and require long-term energy management.

Understanding the AI Energy Family helps students recognize that artificial intelligence has real-world resource implications. It is not only about performance and speed, but also about sustainability, efficiency, and responsible use of technology.

In simple terms, if watts measure how fast energy is used, energy measures how much is used over time.

AI Energy Family Breakdown Chart

Component	Role	Description	Example
Energy	Total Consumption	The total amount of power used over a period of time	Running an AI system for hours or days
Kilowatt-hour (kWh)	Energy Measurement	Unit used to measure energy consumption over time	1 kWh = using 1,000 watts for 1 hour
Energy Usage	Consumption Tracking	Total energy required for AI operations	Training a large model
Training Energy	Learning Cost	Energy used during model training processes	Weeks of GPU usage
Inference Energy	Response Cost	Energy used when AI generates outputs	Answering a user prompt

Component	Role	Description	Example
Energy Efficiency	Optimization Goal	Reducing energy use while maintaining performance	Efficient AI models
Energy Scaling	Growth Impact	Increase in energy use as systems grow larger	Bigger models = more energy
Data Center Energy	Infrastructure Demand	Total energy used by large AI facilities	Server farms operating 24/7
Cooling Energy	Temperature Control	Energy required to cool systems and prevent overheating	Air conditioning in data centers
Renewable Energy	Sustainability Source	Use of clean energy to power AI systems	Solar, wind-powered data centers
Carbon Impact	Environmental Effect	Emissions associated with energy consumption	AI training carbon footprint
Energy Management	Resource Control	Strategies to monitor and reduce energy use	Efficient scheduling, hardware optimization

The AI Energy Family reminds us that artificial intelligence operates within the physical world, where every computation consumes energy and every system has an impact on resources and sustainability.

Energy Family (Total Power Consumption of Artificial Intelligence)

Definition

The **Energy Family** represents the total amount of electricity used by artificial intelligence systems over time. It is measured in watt-hours (Wh) or kilowatt-hours (kWh) and shows how much energy AI systems consume while running.

Energy Scale

1 Watt-hour (Wh)
10 Watt-hours (Wh)
100 Watt-hours (Wh)
500 Watt-hours (Wh)
1,000 Watt-hours (1 Kilowatt-hour, kWh)
10,000 Watt-hours (10 kWh)
100,000 Watt-hours (100 kWh)
1,000,000 Watt-hours (1 Megawatt-hour, MWh)
10,000,000 Watt-hours (10 MWh)
100,000,000+ Watt-hours (100+ MWh)

Key Characteristics

Measured over time (not instant like watts)

Represents total electricity consumption

Increases the longer AI systems run

Directly related to cost and energy usage

Closely connected to Watts Family, Chip Family, and Infrastructure Family

Examples

Low energy → short AI tasks or small devices

Medium energy → daily AI usage on computers

High energy → training AI models and running data centers

Summary

The **Energy Family** provides a numerical representation of the total electricity consumed by artificial intelligence systems over time, helping to illustrate the overall cost and impact of AI operations.

🧠 Student Insight

Energy shows how much total power AI has used over time.

AI Infrastructure Family Introduction

The AI Infrastructure Family represents the large-scale systems and environments that support, power, and connect artificial intelligence technologies. While individual components such as chips, data, and models explain how AI works, infrastructure explains where and how these systems operate in the real world.

AI infrastructure includes data centers, cloud platforms, networking systems, and storage environments that allow artificial intelligence to function at scale. These systems provide the computing power, data access, and connectivity needed to train models, process information, and deliver results to users around the world.

Modern AI systems rely heavily on cloud-based infrastructure, where thousands of machines work together to handle massive workloads. This allows AI to scale efficiently, making it possible to process large datasets, run complex models, and serve millions of users simultaneously. Infrastructure also ensures reliability, security, and continuous availability of AI services.

The AI Infrastructure Family works closely with the Chip Family, which provides the hardware, the Watts and Energy Families, which manage power consumption, and the Data Family, which supplies the information being processed. It also supports the AI Architecture Family by providing the environment where all system components are deployed and connected.

Understanding the AI Infrastructure Family helps students recognize that artificial intelligence is not contained within a single device. Instead, it operates across global systems that require coordination, resources, and engineering to function effectively.

In simple terms, if AI is the system and chips are the engines, infrastructure is the environment that allows everything to run at scale.

AI Infrastructure Family Breakdown Chart

Component	Role	Description	Example
AI Infrastructure	System Environment	The physical and digital systems that support AI operations	Global AI platforms
Data Center	Processing Hub	Facilities that house servers and computing equipment	Large server farms
Cloud Computing	Scalable Platform	Remote systems that provide computing resources over the internet	AWS, Azure, Google Cloud
Servers	Compute Units	Machines that process data and run AI models	Rack-mounted servers
Networking	Connectivity System	Systems that allow communication between machines	Internet, fiber networks
Storage Systems	Data Management	Systems that store large volumes of data	Databases, cloud storage
Distributed Computing	Workload Sharing	Splitting tasks across multiple machines for efficiency	Parallel processing across clusters
Edge Infrastructure	Local Processing	Running AI closer to the user or device	Smart devices, IoT systems
Load Balancing	Traffic Control	Distributes workloads to prevent overload	Managing user requests
Security Systems	Protection Layer	Safeguards data and systems from threats	Encryption, firewalls
Redundancy	Reliability System	Backup systems to ensure continuous operation	Failover servers

Component	Role	Description	Example
Scalability	Growth Capability	Ability to expand resources as demand increases	Adding more servers dynamically

The AI Infrastructure Family reveals that artificial intelligence operates on a global scale, relying on interconnected systems that provide the power, storage, and connectivity needed to support intelligent technologies.

AI Agent Family Introduction

The AI Agent Family represents systems that can take action, make decisions, and perform tasks on behalf of users or other systems. Unlike traditional AI models that only respond to input, AI agents are designed to operate with a level of autonomy, allowing them to plan, execute, and adapt to achieve specific goals.

An AI agent receives input from its environment, processes that information, and takes actions based on predefined objectives or learned behaviors. These actions can include answering questions, automating workflows, retrieving information, or interacting with other systems. Some agents operate in simple environments, while others function in complex systems that require continuous decision-making.

AI agents often combine multiple foundational families. They use the Data Family to gather information, the Memory and Knowledge Families to retain and understand context, and the Neural Network and Parameter Families to process and learn from interactions. They also rely on the AI Architecture and Infrastructure Families to operate reliably at scale.

Modern AI agents can work independently or as part of larger systems. For example, a customer support agent can respond to inquiries automatically, while a more advanced agent can complete multi-step tasks such as scheduling, research, or system management.

Understanding the AI Agent Family helps students see that artificial intelligence is not only about generating responses, but also about taking meaningful action in real-world scenarios.

In simple terms, if AI models think and respond, AI agents act and execute.

AI Agent Family Breakdown Chart

Component	Role	Description	Example
AI Agent	Action System	An AI system that can make decisions and perform tasks	Virtual assistant

Component	Role	Description	Example
Environment	Operating Context	The space where the agent interacts and gathers information	Web, apps, databases
Input Perception	Data Intake	Receives information from the environment	User query or sensor input
Decision Engine	Action Selection	Determines what action to take based on input	Choosing a response or task
Action Execution	Task Performance	Carries out decisions in the environment	Sending an email, retrieving data
Goal System	Objective Setting	Defines what the agent is trying to achieve	Complete a task or solve a problem
Planning Module	Strategy Builder	Breaks down tasks into steps	Multi-step problem solving
Feedback Loop	Learning Cycle	Improves performance based on outcomes	Adjusting actions over time
Autonomy Level	Independence Scale	Degree of independence in decision-making	Fully automated vs assisted
Multi-Agent System	Collaboration Network	Multiple agents working together	Coordinated AI systems

Ingredient Family Introduction

The Ingredient Family represents the essential components that come together to create an artificial intelligence system. Just as a recipe requires specific ingredients to produce a final dish, AI systems rely on a combination of foundational elements working together to function effectively.

Artificial intelligence is not built from a single component. It requires data to learn from, algorithms to guide processing, models to perform tasks, hardware to execute computations, and energy to power the entire system. Each of these elements plays a critical role, and the absence of any one component would prevent the system from operating properly.

The Ingredient Family provides a simplified way for students to understand AI as a system made up of interconnected parts. Instead of viewing AI as complex or mysterious, learners can begin to see it as something constructed from identifiable and understandable components.

This family connects directly with all other foundational families, including Data, Algorithm, Neural Network, Parameter, Chip, and Energy Families. It serves as an overview that brings these elements together into a unified perspective.

Understanding the Ingredient Family helps students recognize that artificial intelligence is built, not magical. It is the result of carefully combining the right components in the right way.

In simple terms, if AI is the final product, the Ingredient Family represents everything needed to build it.

Ingredient Family Breakdown Chart

Component	Role	Description	Example
Data	Learning Input	Provides the information AI uses to learn patterns	Text, images, audio
Algorithms	Instruction Set	Guides how data is processed and decisions are made	Sorting, classification
AI Models	Execution System	Performs tasks such as prediction or generation	Language models
Neural Networks	Processing Structure	Organizes how data is processed through layers	Deep learning models
Parameters	Learning Adjustments	Fine-tune how the model learns and makes predictions	Weights and biases
Tokens	Language Units	Breaks text into smaller pieces for processing	Words or subwords
Hardware (Chips)	Computation Engine	Executes calculations required by AI systems	GPUs, CPUs
Energy	Power Source	Supplies the energy needed to run systems	Electricity usage
Infrastructure	Support System	Provides the environment for AI to operate at scale	Cloud systems, data centers
Memory	Storage System	Stores and retrieves information for processing	Context memory
Knowledge	Understanding Layer	Represents meaning and relationships within data	Knowledge graphs

The Ingredient Family shows that artificial intelligence is built from a combination of essential components, each playing a vital role in creating intelligent systems.

The Frontend and Backend Family of Artificial Intelligence

How AI Systems Connect User Interaction to Intelligent Processing

Introduction

Every artificial intelligence system operates through two essential layers: the frontend and the backend. These layers work together to transform human interaction into intelligent responses, allowing AI systems to function smoothly and effectively.

The frontend is the part of the system that users see and interact with. It includes screens, input tools, and the display of results. Whether a user is typing a question, speaking a command, or uploading an image, all interaction begins at the frontend.

Behind the scenes, the backend serves as the processing engine of the system. It receives input from the frontend, manages data, connects to the AI model, and performs the computations needed to generate a response. The backend is where the intelligence of the system operates, using models, algorithms, and infrastructure to interpret and respond to user requests.

This visual illustrates how these two layers work together as a complete system. It shows the flow of information from user input to AI processing and back to the user as a result. By understanding this structure, students can see that AI is not a single tool, but a coordinated system of layers working together.

In simple terms, the frontend is where interaction happens, and the backend is where intelligence is created.

Every AI system has two sides: what you see and what actually does the thinking.

This structure helps students understand how every interaction with AI is supported by a hidden system of processing and intelligence.

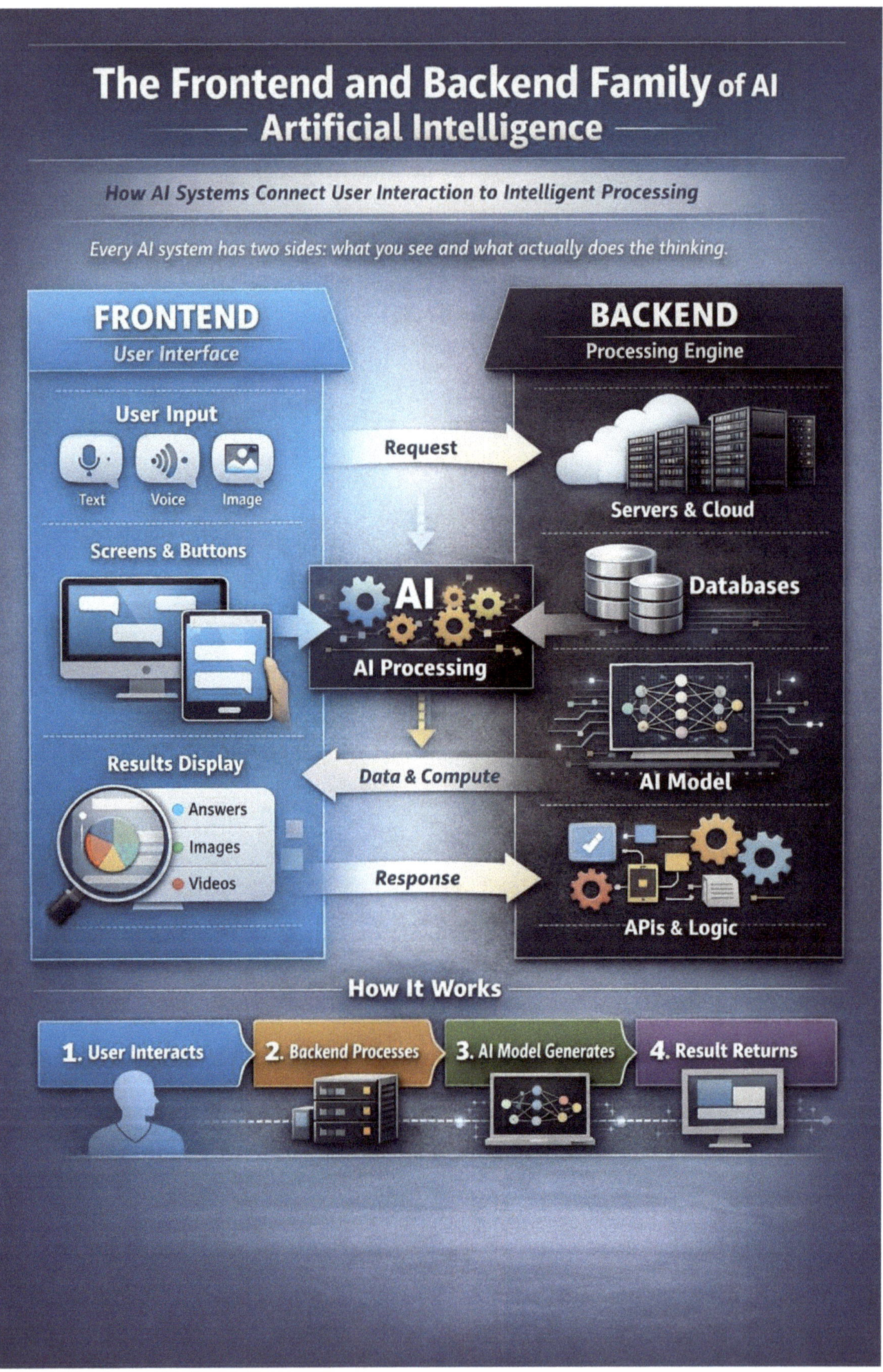

The Frontend and Backend Family of AI
Artificial Intelligence
How AI Systems Connect User Interaction to Intelligent Processing
Every AI system has two sides: what you see and what actually does the thinking.
FRONTEND
User Interface
BACKEND
Processing Engine
User Input
Text
Voice
Image
Request
Servers & Cloud
Screens & Buttons
AI
AI Processing
Databases
Data & Compute
AI Model
Results Display
Answers
Images
Videos
Response
APIs & Logic
How It Works
1. User Interacts
2. Backend Processes
3. AI Model Generates
4. Result Returns

AI Qubit Family Introduction

The AI Qubit Family represents the foundation of quantum computing as it relates to artificial intelligence. While traditional computing relies on bits, which can exist as either 0 or 1, quantum computing uses qubits, which can exist in multiple states simultaneously.

A qubit is the basic unit of quantum information. Unlike classical bits, qubits can take advantage of properties such as superposition and entanglement, allowing quantum systems to process complex computations more efficiently in certain scenarios. This opens new possibilities for solving problems that are difficult or impossible for traditional computers.

In the context of artificial intelligence, qubits have the potential to accelerate learning processes, optimize large-scale systems, and improve complex simulations. Although quantum AI is still in development, it represents a future direction where computational power can expand beyond current limitations.

The AI Qubit Family connects with the Chip Family, as quantum processors are specialized hardware, and with the Algorithm Family, where new types of quantum algorithms are designed. It also relates to the Parameter and Neural Network Families, as researchers explore quantum-enhanced learning models.

Understanding the AI Qubit Family helps students see that artificial intelligence is continuously evolving. It introduces the idea that the foundations of computing themselves can change, leading to new forms of intelligence and problem-solving.

In simple terms, if bits are the foundation of today's computing, qubits represent the foundation of tomorrow's possibilities.

AI Qubit Family Breakdown Chart

Component	Role	Description	Example
Qubit	Quantum Unit	Basic unit of quantum information	Quantum bit in a quantum computer
Superposition	Multi-State Ability	Ability to exist in multiple states at once	0 and 1 simultaneously
Entanglement	Connection Property	Linking qubits so they influence each other	Paired quantum states
Quantum Gate	Operation System	Performs operations on qubits	Quantum logic gates
Quantum Circuit	Processing Structure	Sequence of quantum operations	Quantum algorithms
Quantum Processor	Hardware Engine	Specialized chip for quantum computing	Quantum computer hardware

Component	Role	Description	Example
Quantum Algorithm	Computation Method	Algorithm designed for quantum systems	Optimization problems
Quantum Speedup	Performance Advantage	Faster processing for certain problems	Complex simulations
Quantum Noise	Stability Challenge	Errors caused by environmental interference	Qubit instability
Quantum Error Correction	Stability Solution	Techniques to reduce errors in quantum systems	Fault-tolerant computing

The AI Qubit Family introduces a new frontier in computing, where the limits of traditional systems are expanded, opening the door to more powerful and advanced forms of artificial intelligence.

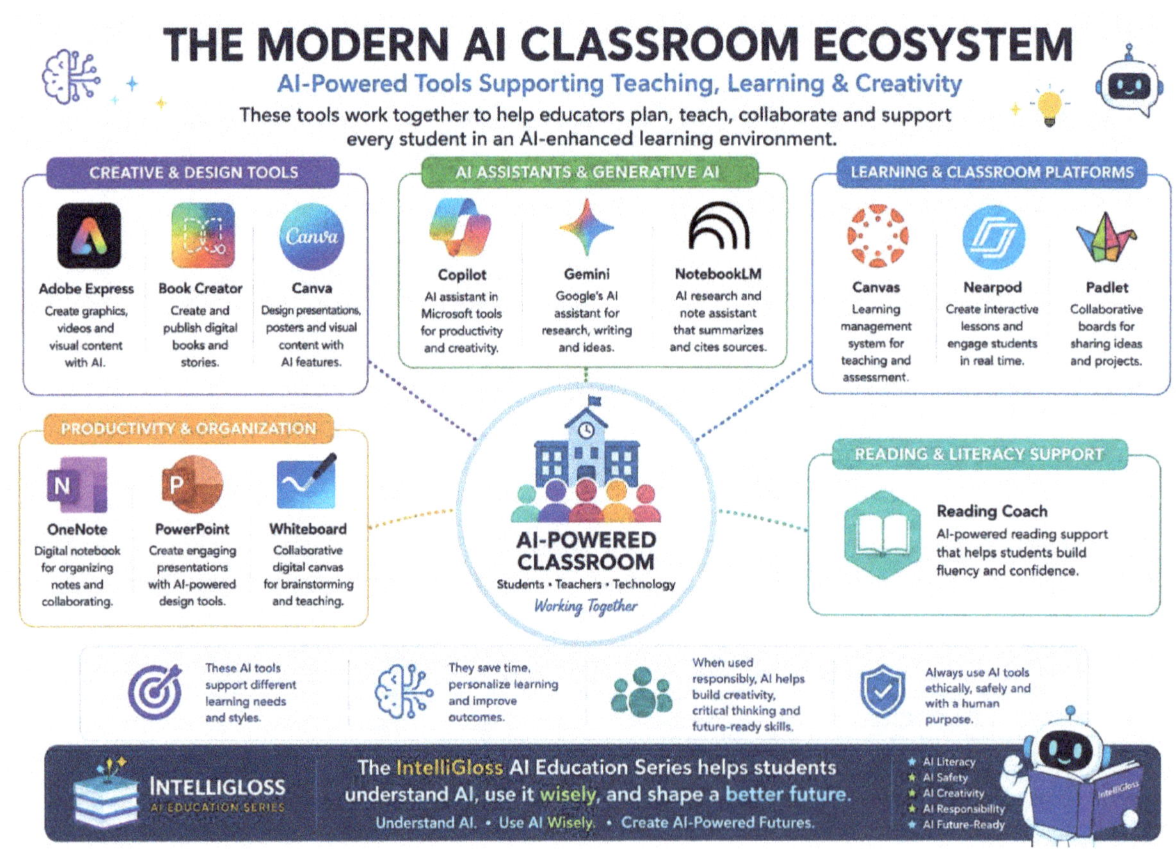

Title:

Data: Fuel for Artificial Neurons
How Information Powers Intelligent Machines

TABLE OF CONTENTS

Introduction

Data: Fuel for Artificial Neurons

How Information Powers Intelligent Machines

In the modern world, data is everywhere. Every text message, online search, photo, video, sensor reading, voice command, social media post, and digital transaction creates data. Behind every intelligent machine, recommendation system, chatbot, search engine, self-driving car, and AI assistant is one powerful force working silently in the background: data.

Data is the fuel that powers artificial intelligence.

Just as the human brain learns from experiences, observations, sounds, images, and memories, artificial intelligence systems learn from data. Machines cannot think, learn, predict, or recognize patterns without information flowing into their artificial neurons. Data feeds the digital brain of modern AI systems and allows machines to improve over time.

But data alone is not enough.

Raw information must be collected, cleaned, organized, processed, and transformed into something machines can understand. Intelligent systems depend on high-quality data to make accurate decisions. Poor data can lead to errors, unfair outcomes, bias, misinformation, and unreliable AI behavior. This is why understanding data is one of the most important foundations of AI literacy.

This book explores how information moves through intelligent systems and how artificial neurons use data to learn patterns, solve problems, and make predictions. Students will discover how machines process numbers, images, text, sounds, and signals to recognize speech, recommend videos, detect fraud, assist doctors, power robotics, and support modern society.

Throughout this book, readers will learn about:

how data becomes knowledge,

how neural networks consume information,

why training data matters,

how cloud systems manage massive datasets,

why ethics and privacy are essential,

and how future technologies such as synthetic data and quantum datasets may transform artificial intelligence forever.

This book also teaches an important truth:

Artificial intelligence is not magic.

Behind every AI system are human-created datasets, algorithms, infrastructure, engineers, educators, and ethical decisions. AI systems only become intelligent because humans teach them through information.

As students move through these chapters, they will begin to understand that data is more than numbers stored inside computers. Data is the bridge between human knowledge and machine intelligence. It allows intelligent systems to learn from the world and respond to human needs in ways that were once impossible.

The future of AI will belong to those who understand not only how to use technology, but also how information shapes intelligent machines.

The goal of this book is to help students, educators, and future innovators understand how data powers artificial neurons and how intelligent systems are built responsibly in the modern age.

Welcome to the world where information becomes intelligence.

— IntelliGloss AI Education Series

Chapter 1: The Lifeblood of AI — Understanding Data

In the vast digital world, every intelligent system—whether it's a simple chatbot, a self-driving car, or a supercomputer—relies on one essential element: **data**. Data is the lifeblood that gives life and purpose to artificial intelligence. Without it, machines would remain empty shells, incapable of learning, reasoning, or adapting. Just as humans depend on experience and knowledge to make decisions, machines depend on data to understand the world around them.

When we speak about *data*, we are referring to the raw facts, numbers, symbols, and observations that are collected from the environment. In its simplest form, data can be something as small as a single temperature reading or as complex as millions of sentences written in different languages. Artificial intelligence systems are built to process these bits of information and transform them into understanding. This transformation is what allows machines to simulate intelligent behavior.

The relationship between **data and intelligence** mirrors the relationship between **food and energy**. Just as food fuels the human body, data fuels artificial neurons. When we eat, our body converts nutrients into energy, enabling us to think, move, and grow. Similarly, when a machine "consumes" data, it extracts patterns and insights that allow it to learn and evolve. The more data it receives—and the higher the quality of that data—the more refined and capable it becomes.

However, not all data is created equal. Machines can only learn effectively when the data is accurate, diverse, and relevant. If the data is biased or incomplete, the intelligence that emerges will reflect those flaws. This is why the foundation of AI learning begins not just with gathering large amounts of data, but with ensuring that the data represents truth and fairness. In classrooms, this idea helps students understand why information ethics and accuracy are so important in the digital age.

Another way to think about data is as the **language of the machine mind**. Humans use spoken and written words to communicate ideas. Machines, on the other hand, use data to communicate and understand the world. Every image, sound, or text that an AI system encounters becomes a message written in this universal digital language. By interpreting millions of these messages, artificial neurons gradually form a mental model of reality.

Imagine teaching a child to recognize animals. The child learns by seeing thousands of examples—cats, dogs, birds—and over time, begins to understand the differences and similarities. Machines learn in exactly the same way. They don't possess emotions or experiences, but they build understanding through repeated exposure to labeled data. This process, known as **machine learning**, allows AI systems to grow more accurate with each new piece of information.

In this sense, data is more than just a resource—it is **the foundation of machine cognition**. Without data, the most powerful neural network would remain motionless, unable to activate even a single artificial neuron. With the right data, however, those same neurons begin to spark to life, forming connections that mimic the intricate pathways of the human brain.

Understanding the value of data helps students appreciate how deeply information is tied to the modern world. Every search, photo, and message contributes to the immense ocean of data that fuels AI research and development. As learners and digital citizens, students will come to see that handling data with care and responsibility is not just a technical skill—it's a moral and social duty.

As we move deeper into this book, we will explore how data flows through networks, how it's processed, cleaned, visualized, and protected. Students will learn that data is not merely information—it is **the energy source of the intelligent age**. In the chapters ahead, the story of data becomes the story of artificial neurons learning to see, hear, and understand the world—one byte at a time.

Chapter 1 Reflection

Understanding data is the first step in understanding artificial intelligence. This chapter explains that AI does not think, feel, or learn on its own. It depends entirely on data to function. Just as humans learn from experiences, machines learn from information collected from the world. Reflecting on this idea helps students realize that AI systems are shaped by the data they are given.

Students should consider how often they create data in their daily lives—through searches, messages, photos, and online activities. Each action adds to the digital world that AI systems learn from. This reflection encourages students to think about their responsibility as digital citizens. If data is inaccurate or biased, AI systems may make unfair or harmful decisions.

This chapter also invites students to reflect on the ethical importance of data. Since data influences how AI understands the world, humans must take responsibility for how data is collected, shared, and used. Understanding data is not just about technology—it is about values, fairness, and accountability in an intelligent society.

Chapter 1 Summary

Data is the foundation of all artificial intelligence systems. AI cannot learn, reason, or adapt without data. Data includes raw facts such as numbers, images, sounds, text, and observations collected from the world. AI systems process this information to identify patterns and make decisions.

The chapter compares data to food for the human body. Just as food provides energy, data provides intelligence. The quality of data matters just as much as the quantity. Biased or incomplete data leads to flawed AI outcomes.

Data also acts as the language of machines. While humans communicate through words, machines communicate through data. By analyzing large amounts of information, AI systems build models that help them understand and respond to the world. Understanding data helps students see why accuracy, fairness, and responsibility are essential in the age of artificial intelligence.

Chapter 1 Quiz

1. What is described as the lifeblood of artificial intelligence?
2. What is data in its simplest form?
3. Why is data compared to food for the human body?
4. What happens when AI systems are trained on biased or incomplete data?
5. How do machines use data to learn?
6. Why is data called the language of machines?
7. How is machine learning similar to how children learn?
8. Can AI function without data? Explain why or why not.
9. Why is data accuracy important in AI systems?
10. What responsibility do students have as digital citizens when it comes to data?

Chapter 1 Worksheet

Part A: Short Response

1. In your own words, explain why data is essential for artificial intelligence.
2. Give one real-life example of data that AI systems might use.
3. Explain what could happen if an AI system learns from unfair or incorrect data.

Part B: Critical Thinking

4. Think about your daily online activities. List two ways you create data.
5. Why do you think data responsibility is considered a moral issue, not just a technical one?

Part C: Reflection

6. How does understanding data change the way you think about AI systems you use every day?

Chapter 1 Answer Key

Quiz Answers

1. Data
2. Raw facts, numbers, symbols, or observations
3. Because data fuels AI systems just as food fuels the human body
4. The AI may produce unfair, inaccurate, or harmful results
5. By analyzing patterns and learning from repeated examples
6. Because machines use data to understand and communicate information
7. Both learn by seeing many examples over time
8. No, because AI needs data to learn and make decisions
9. Because inaccurate data leads to incorrect or biased outcomes
10. Students must use, share, and create data responsibly

Worksheet Sample Answers
(Answers may vary)

1. Data gives AI information to learn and make decisions.
2. Photos, search results, messages, or sensor readings.
3. The AI may make wrong or unfair decisions.
4. Searching online, posting on social media, sending messages.
5. Because data affects people's lives and fairness in society.
6. It helps students realize AI decisions depend on human-created data.

Chapter 2: From Information to Insight — The Journey of Data

Every piece of data begins its life as a simple observation — a number, a sound, a color, or a word. On its own, this small fragment of information may not seem meaningful. Yet, when collected, organized, and analyzed, it becomes the foundation of intelligence. The journey from raw information to insightful understanding is what makes artificial intelligence both powerful and human-like in its learning process.

In human terms, we might think of this journey as the way our brains transform experiences into knowledge. When we see, hear, or read something new, our mind records the details. Over time, these details form connections, and those connections create understanding. Machines follow a similar path. They start by **collecting data**, then **cleaning and organizing it**, and finally **learning from it** until patterns emerge that allow them to make predictions or decisions.

The first step in this process is **data collection**. Machines gather information from countless sources — sensors, cameras, websites, documents, or human input. For example, an AI weather model collects temperature readings, wind speeds, and humidity levels from thousands of sensors around the world. Each individual piece of data contributes to a larger picture. The more accurate and diverse the collection, the stronger the foundation for intelligent insight.

Once the data is collected, it must go through a phase called **data cleaning**. Just like students proofreading an essay, machines must remove mistakes, duplicates, and irrelevant pieces of information. In this stage, engineers check for errors, missing values, and inconsistencies. Clean data ensures that the AI learns correctly, without being misled by noise or false signals. In education, this step teaches students the importance of critical thinking — learning to separate fact from confusion before drawing conclusions.

The next phase is **data organization and preprocessing**. Here, data is structured into a form that the AI system can understand. Numbers may be normalized, text converted into tokens, and images turned into arrays of pixels. This transformation makes it easier for the machine to identify patterns. Think of it like arranging puzzle pieces on a table before beginning to assemble the picture — organization allows the pattern to reveal itself.

After organization comes the most transformative stage: **data analysis and learning**. Artificial neurons begin processing the data, searching for recurring patterns. They start to notice relationships between inputs and outputs — for instance, recognizing that certain weather conditions often lead to rain, or that certain words appear together in similar sentences. Over time, these relationships turn into models that represent real-world understanding. This is the moment when **information becomes insight**.

The insights discovered through data are the reason AI systems appear intelligent. When an AI assistant predicts the next word you will type, or when a recommendation system suggests a movie you might like, those actions are the result of countless insights drawn from massive amounts of data. These insights are not guesses; they are carefully learned patterns that help machines anticipate what might come next.

However, insight alone is not enough. For an AI system to be truly useful, it must also be **interpretable**. This means humans should be able to understand how the AI arrived at its conclusion. In the classroom, this concept is vital. Students should learn not only to trust intelligent systems but also to question and analyze their reasoning. Transparent insight leads to responsible technology.

As we progress in this book, students will come to see that every intelligent decision begins with data's long journey from chaos to clarity. Teachers can use this chapter to help students reflect on how their own learning mirrors that of the machine: they gather knowledge, organize it, clean it, and eventually transform it into understanding. The beauty of this parallel is that both humans and machines thrive on information — but it is insight that transforms them from passive learners into thinkers.

The journey of data is, therefore, more than a technical process. It is a story of transformation — from numbers into knowledge, from patterns into perception, and from information into intelligence. In the next chapter, we will travel deeper into the core of machine learning to discover how **neurons and numbers** work together to feed the brain of artificial intelligence.

Chapter 2 Reflection

This chapter helps students understand that data does not become useful the moment it is collected. Data must travel through several important steps before it turns into insight. Just like humans learn by organizing experiences and thinking about them, machines learn by cleaning, organizing, and analyzing data.

Students are encouraged to reflect on how their own learning mirrors the learning process of artificial intelligence. When students gather information, remove mistakes, organize ideas, and look for patterns, they are following the same journey as data inside an AI system. This reflection helps students realize that intelligence—human or artificial—is not about memorizing facts, but about understanding relationships and meaning.

This chapter also invites students to think about responsibility. Since humans control how data is collected and processed, they play a major role in shaping the insights AI systems produce. Reflection on this process teaches students to be thoughtful, critical, and ethical users of intelligent technology.

Chapter 2 Summary

Data begins as simple information that has little meaning on its own. Through a structured journey—collection, cleaning, organization, and analysis—data is transformed into insight. This transformation allows artificial intelligence systems to recognize patterns, make predictions, and support decision-making.

The chapter explains how AI learning is similar to human learning. Both humans and machines gather information, organize it, remove errors, and connect ideas over time. Data cleaning ensures accuracy, while organization makes patterns easier to detect.

The final stage of the journey is insight, where AI systems discover meaningful relationships within data. These insights power everyday technologies such as recommendation systems, predictive tools, and digital assistants. Understanding this journey helps students see why transparency, accuracy, and responsible data use are essential in artificial intelligence.

Chapter 2 Quiz

1. What does data start as before it becomes insight?
2. Why is data cleaning important in the AI learning process?
3. How is AI learning similar to human learning?
4. What happens during data organization and preprocessing?
5. Why is collecting diverse and accurate data important?
6. What is meant by "insight" in artificial intelligence?
7. Give one example of how AI uses insight in everyday life.
8. Why should AI insights be understandable to humans?
9. What role do artificial neurons play in learning from data?
10. Why is the journey of data considered a transformation?

Chapter 2 Worksheet

Part A: Understanding the Process

1. List the main stages of the data journey described in this chapter.
2. Explain why raw data is not very useful on its own.

Part B: Critical Thinking

3. Describe how organizing information helps both students and machines learn better.
4. What problems could happen if data is not cleaned before analysis?

Part C: Reflection

5. Think about how you study for a test. Which steps match the data journey in AI?
6. Why do you think transparency is important when AI makes decisions?

Chapter 2 Answer Key

Quiz Answers

1. Simple observations or raw information
2. To remove errors, duplicates, and misleading information
3. Both collect information, organize it, remove mistakes, and find patterns
4. Data is structured into a form the AI system can understand
5. Because better data leads to more accurate and fair insights
6. Insight is meaningful understanding gained from patterns in data
7. Movie recommendations, weather predictions, or word suggestions
8. So humans can trust, question, and use AI responsibly
9. They process data and search for patterns
10. Because data changes from simple facts into meaningful understanding

Worksheet Sample Answers

(Answers may vary)

1. Collection, cleaning, organization, analysis, and insight.
2. Raw data has no meaning until it is processed and analyzed.
3. Organization helps ideas connect and patterns become clear.
4. AI could learn incorrect or biased information.
5. Gathering notes, removing mistakes, organizing ideas, reviewing patterns.
6. Transparency helps people understand and trust AI decisions.

Chapter 3: Neurons and Numbers — Feeding the Brain of Machines

When we think of the human brain, we imagine billions of tiny neurons communicating through electrical signals. Each neuron receives information, processes it, and passes it along to others. Together, these neurons create thought, memory, and decision-making. In artificial intelligence, the same idea exists — only instead of biological cells, we use **artificial neurons**. These digital counterparts are mathematical models that process numbers instead of electrical impulses, yet their purpose is remarkably similar: to learn, adapt, and make sense of the world.

WHAT ARE ARTIFICIAL NEURONS?

Artificial neurons are the basic building blocks of artificial intelligence. They are designed to imitate how the human brain works, but instead of using biological cells, they use mathematics. Each artificial neuron receives information, processes it, and then passes it on to other neurons.

In the human brain, neurons communicate through electrical signals. In AI systems, artificial neurons communicate using numbers. Even though they are not alive, they perform a similar role — helping the system learn from information and make decisions.

You can think of an artificial neuron as a tiny decision-maker. It looks at the information it receives and decides what is important and what is not. When many of these neurons work together, they create a system that can recognize patterns, solve problems, and improve over time.

At the heart of every intelligent system lies a **neural network**, a vast structure of artificial neurons connected through layers. Each neuron acts as a small decision-maker, receiving inputs, multiplying them by weights, and passing the result through an activation function. In simpler terms, every neuron looks at the data, decides what's important, and contributes its understanding to the next layer. These layers work together like teams in a company — each one specializing in part of the problem until the final decision emerges at the output layer.

NEURAL NETWORKS EXPLAINED

A neural network is a system made up of many artificial neurons working together. These neurons are arranged in layers, and each layer has a specific role in processing information.

The first layer is called the input layer. This is where data enters the system. The data then moves through one or more hidden layers, where the neurons analyze and transform the information. Finally, the processed data reaches the output layer, where the system produces a result.

Each layer builds on the work of the previous one. Just like a team working on a project, each group of neurons focuses on a specific part of the task. By the time the information reaches the final layer, the system has combined all of its learning to make a decision or prediction.

Neural networks allow machines to handle complex tasks such as recognizing images, understanding language, and making recommendations.

But what do artificial neurons eat? Their diet is made up of **numbers** — the translated form of real-world data. Every image, sound, or word must be converted into numerical values before a machine can understand it. For instance, a digital photo is nothing more than a grid of pixels, each represented by numbers that describe its color and brightness. When an artificial neural network studies this image, it does not see a cat or a dog the way humans do; it sees a pattern of numbers that, through learning, becomes associated with meaning.

WHY MACHINES USE NUMBERS

Machines use numbers because numbers are the only language they can understand. Unlike humans, machines cannot see images, hear sounds, or read words directly. Everything must be converted into numbers before a machine can process it.

For example, a picture is not seen as a face or an object by a machine. Instead, it is seen as a collection of pixels, each represented by numbers that describe color and brightness. Similarly, text is converted into numerical representations, and sound is turned into numerical patterns of frequencies.

Once information becomes numbers, machines can perform mathematical operations on it. These calculations allow the system to find patterns, compare information, and make decisions.

In simple terms, numbers are the bridge between the real world and the machine world.

DATA ENCODING

Data encoding is the process of converting real-world information into numbers that machines can understand. Since machines cannot interpret raw images, sounds, or text, encoding is the step that prepares data for learning.

Different types of data are encoded in different ways. Text can be turned into numerical vectors using techniques like tokenization or word embeddings. Images are converted into grids of numbers representing pixels. Sound is transformed into numerical frequencies that capture patterns in audio.

This process may seem technical, but it is essential. Without encoding, machines would not be able to process or learn from data at all. Encoding ensures that all information is translated into a form that can be analyzed mathematically.

You can think of encoding as translating a human language into a machine language.

The process begins with **data encoding** — the conversion of raw data into numerical form. For text, words are turned into numerical vectors using methods like tokenization or word embeddings. For sound, the vibrations are transformed into sequences of numerical frequencies. And for images, pixels become arrays of numbers. This translation is essential because machines can only perform mathematical operations, not emotional or visual interpretations like humans. Once data is transformed into numbers, the neural network can begin its work.

Each neuron multiplies its input numbers by a set of **weights** — values that determine the importance of each input. A high weight means the neuron pays more attention to that input, while a low weight means it's less relevant. After adding these weighted values together, the neuron passes the sum through an **activation function**, which decides whether that neuron "fires." This process resembles how biological neurons activate when electrical signals reach a certain threshold. In essence, numbers are the sparks that ignite artificial neurons.

HOW NEURONS LEARN

Artificial neurons learn by adjusting how they respond to information. When a neural network processes data, it makes a prediction or decision. If the result is incorrect, the system measures the error and makes adjustments to improve.

These adjustments happen by changing values called weights. Weights determine how important each piece of information is. When the system makes mistakes, it updates these weights so that the next prediction is more accurate.

NUMBERS CREATE KNOWLEDGE

Numbers are more than just symbols in artificial intelligence — they are the foundation of learning. When machines process large amounts of numerical data, they begin to discover patterns and relationships.

These patterns allow the system to make sense of information. For example, by analyzing numbers from thousands of images, a machine can learn to recognize objects. By studying numerical patterns in language, it can learn to understand and generate text.

This process shows that knowledge in AI is built from numbers. Just as humans learn from experiences, machines learn from data represented as numbers.

In this way, numbers become the building blocks of intelligence. They allow machines to move beyond simple calculations and develop the ability to predict, classify, and respond to the world around them.

This learning process is repeated many times. With each cycle, the system becomes better at recognizing patterns and making correct decisions. This method of learning from mistakes is similar to how humans improve through practice and feedback.

Over time, the network becomes more refined, turning simple calculations into intelligent behavior.

Through repeated exposure to examples, the network adjusts its weights to improve accuracy — a process known as **learning**. If the output is wrong, the system measures the error and uses algorithms like **backpropagation** to correct itself. This cycle of feeding data, producing results, and adjusting weights continues until the network achieves the desired level of intelligence. Over time, what started as random numbers evolves into a structured system capable of recognizing faces, predicting weather, or translating languages.

This learning process reveals something extraordinary: **numbers create knowledge**. In the same way that human experience builds understanding, numerical data builds artificial intelligence. When we feed a neural network with thousands of examples, it begins to "understand" in its own mathematical way. It doesn't feel or think as humans do, but it identifies relationships that humans might never see. This is why data truly acts as the fuel — it is what keeps the engine of learning alive.

Teachers can use this concept to help students appreciate the link between math and intelligence. Every equation in a neural network represents a small thought in the digital brain. When students learn how weights, biases, and activation functions interact, they're not just learning numbers —

they're discovering how machines think. This connection transforms mathematics from an abstract subject into a living language of reasoning and logic.

In the end, artificial neurons and numbers form a partnership that defines modern AI. Data enters as simple information, numbers bring it to life, and neurons transform it into understanding. As we continue to explore deeper layers of AI, we'll see how these tiny digital brains work together to learn from experience, correct their mistakes, and build knowledge — just as living brains do in the classroom of life.

In the next chapter, we will explore this fascinating process of learning in greater depth — uncovering **how machines learn**, and how repetition, feedback, and correction allow artificial neurons to grow smarter with every cycle of training.

Chapter 3 Summary

Artificial intelligence is powered by artificial neurons, which are mathematical models inspired by the human brain. These neurons work together in neural networks to process information and make decisions. Unlike humans, machines do not see images or hear sounds directly. Instead, all information must first be converted into numbers.

Data encoding transforms text, sound, and images into numerical values that machines can understand. Artificial neurons multiply these numbers by weights, combine them, and pass them through activation functions to decide what information is important. Through repeated training, neural networks adjust their weights to reduce errors and improve accuracy.

This learning process shows how numbers create knowledge in artificial intelligence. By processing large amounts of numerical data, neural networks can recognize patterns, make predictions, and support intelligent behavior. Understanding neurons and numbers helps students see how math becomes the foundation of machine learning.

Chapter 3 Quiz

1. What are artificial neurons modeled after?
2. How are artificial neurons different from biological neurons?
3. Why must all data be converted into numbers before AI can learn?
4. What is the purpose of weights in an artificial neuron?
5. What does an activation function do?
6. What is data encoding?
7. How does a neural network improve when it makes a mistake?
8. What role does repetition play in AI learning?
9. Why are numbers considered the "food" of artificial neurons?
10. How does this chapter connect mathematics to intelligence?

Chapter 3 Worksheet

Part A: Key Concepts

1. Describe in your own words what an artificial neuron does.
2. List three types of data that must be converted into numbers for AI systems.

Part B: Understanding the Process

3. Explain why weights are important in helping a neural network learn.
4. What happens when an AI system produces an incorrect result?

Part C: Reflection

5. Compare how students learn from mistakes to how AI systems learn from errors.
6. Why do you think understanding numbers is important for understanding AI?

Chapter 3 Answer Key

Quiz Answers

1. The human brain's neurons
2. Artificial neurons use math and numbers instead of electrical signals
3. Because machines can only process numerical information
4. They determine how important each input is
5. It decides whether a neuron activates or not
6. The process of converting data into numerical form
7. It adjusts its weights to reduce errors
8. Repetition helps the system improve accuracy over time
9. Because numbers provide the information needed for learning
10. It shows how math allows machines to learn and make decisions

Worksheet Sample Answers

(Answers may vary)

1. An artificial neuron receives numbers, processes them, and sends results forward.
2. Text, sound, and images.
3. Weights help the network focus on important information.
4. The system measures the error and adjusts its settings.
5. Both improve by recognizing mistakes and correcting them.
6. Numbers are the language AI uses to learn and reason.

Chapter 4: How Machines Learn

Learning is the defining characteristic of intelligence — whether in humans, animals, or machines. For a human being, learning is a gradual process of observation, practice, and reflection. We make mistakes, analyze them, and improve over time. Artificial intelligence follows a surprisingly similar path. Machines learn through **experience with data**, using mathematical rules to recognize patterns, make predictions, and adjust their internal understanding.

At the core of machine learning lies a simple idea: the more experience a machine has, the better it becomes at performing a task. In the case of AI, "experience" means **data**. Machines are exposed to thousands or millions of examples, each teaching them something new. For instance, an AI system trained to recognize handwritten numbers might be shown thousands of samples written by different people. Over time, it learns to identify the shapes and patterns that define each number, even when the handwriting is messy or unfamiliar.

LEARNING FROM DATA

Machines learn from data in the same way students learn from examples. Each piece of data provides information that helps the system understand patterns and relationships.

For example, if a machine is learning to recognize animals, it might be shown thousands of images of cats and dogs. By studying these examples, the machine begins to notice differences in shape, size, and features. Over time, it learns how to correctly identify each animal.

The quality and variety of data are very important. If the data is clear and diverse, the machine learns more accurately. If the data is limited or incorrect, the machine may develop misunderstandings. This is why good data leads to better learning.

The process begins with **input data** — the examples given to the machine. These inputs are passed into an algorithm, a set of mathematical rules that define how the machine should learn. The algorithm's goal is to find relationships between inputs and outputs. For example, if the input is an image of a fruit and the correct label is "apple," the algorithm learns what features— such as color, shape, and texture—correspond to that label. Through this process, the machine builds an internal map that connects cause and effect.

THE ROLE OF ALGORITHMS

Algorithms are the instructions that guide how a machine learns from data. They are sets of mathematical rules that help the system find patterns and relationships.

When data is fed into a machine, the algorithm processes it step by step. It looks for connections between inputs and outputs and adjusts its internal structure to improve its predictions.

You can think of an algorithm as a teacher guiding the learning process. It does not give the machine all the answers, but it helps the machine discover patterns on its own. Without algorithms, machines would not know how to learn from data.

WHAT IS MACHINE LEARNING

Machine learning is the process that allows computers to learn from data instead of being directly programmed for every task. Instead of following fixed instructions, machines study examples, find patterns, and improve their performance over time.

Just like humans learn through experience, machines learn by analyzing information. The more examples they see, the better they become at understanding patterns and making decisions. This ability to learn from data is what makes artificial intelligence powerful and adaptable.

In simple terms, machine learning is how machines turn experience into knowledge.

Learning in machines takes several forms, but the three most common are **supervised learning**, **unsupervised learning**, and **reinforcement learning**. In **supervised learning**, the machine learns from labeled data — meaning that every example comes with the correct answer. This is like a teacher guiding a student with clear feedback. The model compares its predictions to the true answers and adjusts itself until its errors are minimized. This method is used in tasks such as image recognition, speech-to-text systems, and spam email detection.

In **unsupervised learning**, the data has no labels or answers. The machine must find hidden patterns on its own. This type of learning mimics curiosity — it's as though the machine is exploring the world and grouping similar things together based on observation. Clustering customer preferences, discovering topics in documents, and finding patterns in medical data are examples of this learning style. It teaches machines to identify structure in chaos.

The third type, **reinforcement learning**, teaches machines through trial and error. Instead of being told what is correct, the machine receives rewards or penalties based on its actions. This approach is used in robotics, gaming, and autonomous vehicles. For example, an AI learning to play chess receives a positive reward when it wins and a negative one when it loses. Over time, it learns which strategies lead to victory. This mirrors the way humans learn from experience and feedback.

A crucial part of the learning process is **error correction**. Machines don't learn perfectly the first time. They make predictions, measure how wrong they are, and adjust their parameters using algorithms like **backpropagation**. This repetition allows the network to gradually reduce its mistakes. Each round of learning strengthens its understanding, much like how students refine their skills through continuous practice.

Behind every machine-learning model lies an invisible teacher called the **loss function**. This function measures how far the machine's predictions are from the correct answers. The smaller the loss, the better the machine is performing. In a sense, the loss function gives feedback to the AI about how much it still has to learn. Students can think of it like receiving a test score — the lower the score, the more room for improvement.

As the training continues, machines begin to **generalize**, meaning they can make correct predictions even on data they have never seen before. This is the moment when artificial intelligence demonstrates true learning — when it moves beyond memorization and starts applying knowledge creatively. It's the same leap humans make when they use past lessons to solve new problems.

Teachers can use this chapter to help students see that **learning is universal** — it's not just for humans. Machines, too, rely on experience, feedback, and correction to grow smarter. Understanding this process also helps students recognize their role as responsible data creators, since every dataset teaches a machine how to think.

In the next chapter, we will explore the inner logic that guides this learning: the **activation functions**, the decision-makers of the neural world. These tiny mathematical thresholds determine whether a neuron "fires," giving artificial intelligence its rhythm, pulse, and decision-making power — the heartbeat of machine learning.

Chapter 4 Reflection

This chapter shows that learning is not exclusive to humans. Machines also learn through experience, repetition, and correction. Artificial intelligence improves over time by studying data, making predictions, and adjusting itself when those predictions are incorrect. Reflecting on this process helps students understand that learning is a gradual journey, not an instant result.

Students are encouraged to think about how mistakes play an important role in learning. Both humans and machines rely on feedback to grow. When a machine receives information about what it did wrong, it uses that feedback to improve future decisions. This mirrors how students learn through practice, reflection, and revision.

This chapter also invites students to reflect on their responsibility in shaping AI. Since machines learn from data created by humans, the quality of that data matters. Understanding how machines learn helps students become more thoughtful, ethical, and aware users of intelligent technology.

Chapter 4 Summary

Machine learning is the process by which artificial intelligence systems improve through experience with data. Just like humans learn by observing, practicing, and correcting mistakes, machines learn by studying examples and adjusting their internal rules. The more data and feedback a machine receives, the better it becomes at performing tasks.

The learning process begins with input data, which is processed by algorithms that search for relationships between inputs and outcomes. Over time, these algorithms build internal models that help the machine recognize patterns and make predictions. Three main types of machine learning guide this process: supervised learning, unsupervised learning, and reinforcement learning.

Supervised learning uses labeled data and clear feedback, similar to a teacher guiding a student. Unsupervised learning allows machines to explore data on their own and discover hidden patterns. Reinforcement learning teaches machines through rewards and penalties, encouraging them to learn from trial and error. Error correction, guided by loss functions, helps machines measure their progress and improve accuracy. When machines begin to generalize—applying what they've learned to new situations—they demonstrate true learning. Understanding this process helps students see how intelligence grows through experience, feedback, and responsibility.

Chapter 4 Quiz

1. What does learning mean for a machine?
2. What role does data play in machine learning?
3. What is an algorithm in simple terms?
4. How does supervised learning work?
5. What makes unsupervised learning different from supervised learning?
6. How does reinforcement learning teach machines?
7. Why are mistakes important in machine learning?
8. What is the purpose of a loss function?
9. What does it mean when a machine can generalize?
10. How is machine learning similar to human learning?

Chapter 4 Worksheet

Part A: Understanding Learning Types

1. Describe supervised learning using your own words.
2. Give one example of where unsupervised learning might be useful.

Part B: Thinking Deeper

3. Explain why feedback is essential for both humans and machines.
4. What could happen if a machine learns from poor-quality data?

Part C: Reflection

5. Compare how you learn from mistakes to how machines learn from errors.
6. Why is it important for students to understand how machines learn?

Chapter 4 Answer Key

Quiz Answers

1. Improving performance by learning from data and experience
2. Data provides examples that teach the machine
3. A set of rules that guides how a machine learns
4. The machine learns from labeled data with correct answers
5. It finds patterns without being given answers
6. Through rewards and penalties based on actions
7. Mistakes show the machine what needs to be corrected
8. To measure how wrong the machine's predictions are
9. It can apply learning to new, unseen data
10. Both learn through experience, feedback, and practice

Worksheet Sample Answers

(Answers may vary)

1. Supervised learning uses examples with correct answers to guide learning.
2. Grouping similar customers or discovering topics in documents.
3. Feedback helps learners understand what to improve.
4. The machine may learn incorrect or biased patterns.
5. Both adjust behavior after recognizing errors.
6. It helps students become informed and responsible AI users.

Chapter 5: Activation Functions — The Neuron's Decision Maker

Every intelligent decision made by a machine begins with a choice — a moment when an artificial neuron decides whether to respond or stay silent. This crucial process is guided by a mathematical tool known as the **activation function**. In many ways, the activation function serves as the **decision-maker** of the artificial neuron, determining how signals move through the network and whether the information being processed is important enough to influence the final outcome.

To understand activation functions, it helps to first imagine how biological neurons work. In the human brain, neurons fire electrical impulses only when they reach a certain threshold. If the signal from other connected neurons is too weak, the neuron remains quiet. But if the signal is strong enough, the neuron activates and sends information forward. Artificial neurons operate in a similar way — except instead of electricity, they use numbers, and instead of firing signals, they apply mathematical formulas.

The activation function is what gives artificial neurons their **nonlinear power**. Without it, a neural network would be like a straight line — predictable, limited, and unable to handle the complex, curved relationships that exist in the real world. Nonlinearity allows AI systems to make sense of things that aren't perfectly organized or evenly spaced. For example, the difference between a cat and a dog isn't just one line of separation; it's a web of overlapping features. Activation functions give machines the flexibility to recognize those patterns.

There are several types of activation functions, each serving a specific purpose. The most common is the **Sigmoid function**, which compresses input values into a range between 0 and 1. This makes it easy to interpret the neuron's output as a probability — a gentle "yes" or "no." Another widely used type is the **ReLU**, short for Rectified Linear Unit. ReLU is simple but powerful: it outputs zero for negative values and passes positive values unchanged. This allows networks to focus on signals that truly matter while ignoring unnecessary noise. Modern AI systems rely heavily on ReLU because it speeds up learning and helps deep networks perform efficiently.

There are also specialized activation functions like **tanh (hyperbolic tangent)**, which outputs values between -1 and 1, and **Softmax**, which is often used in the final layer of classification models. Softmax helps the machine make a clear choice by assigning probabilities that sum to one, allowing it to decide which category an input most likely belongs to — such as whether an image shows a car, a tree, or a person. These different functions act like unique personalities within the neural network, each shaping how the machine thinks and reacts.

In simple terms, the activation function answers one key question: *Should this neuron activate or not?* That single decision, repeated billions of times across thousands of layers, is what gives modern AI its power to recognize speech, translate languages, or predict outcomes. Every "thought" the network produces begins with an activation — a mathematical spark that turns silent data into meaningful signals.

One of the most fascinating aspects of activation functions is how they **mimic biological intelligence**. Just as neurons in the human brain use chemical signals to determine whether to fire, artificial neurons use mathematical thresholds to decide their response. This similarity is what allows AI systems to approximate human-like learning and adapt to different environments. It also explains why neural networks are often described as *the brain's mirror in mathematics*.

Teachers can use this chapter to demonstrate the connection between biology and computation. By comparing the way neurons fire in the brain with how artificial neurons activate through formulas, students gain a deeper appreciation for both neuroscience and computer science. Activities might include plotting activation functions on a graph, experimenting with their shapes, and observing how changing a single function can alter the behavior of an entire network.

Ultimately, activation functions are more than just equations — they represent the heartbeat of learning machines. They decide which signals are heard, which are ignored, and how knowledge grows through layers of interconnected reasoning. Without activation functions, neural networks would be silent — a collection of idle nodes with no capacity to think or respond. With them, data becomes alive, patterns become visible, and intelligence begins to emerge.

In the next chapter, we will explore how machines take the next step in their learning journey through **backpropagation** — the remarkable process that allows artificial neurons to learn from their mistakes and refine their decisions over time.

Chapter 5 Summary

Activation functions are the decision-makers inside artificial neurons. They determine whether the information flowing through a neural network should move forward or be ignored. Without activation functions, neural networks would be unable to handle complex problems because they would only respond in straight, predictable ways.

Artificial neurons work by receiving numerical inputs, combining them, and passing the result through an activation function. This function introduces nonlinearity, allowing the network to recognize complex patterns found in real-world data. Nonlinearity is what allows AI systems to tell the difference between similar objects, sounds, or ideas.

Different activation functions serve different purposes. Sigmoid functions help represent probabilities, ReLU functions allow networks to focus on important signals and learn faster, and Softmax functions help models make clear choices between categories. Together, these functions shape how neural networks think, learn, and respond. Understanding activation functions helps students see how simple mathematical decisions form the foundation of intelligent behavior in machines.

Chapter 5 Quiz

1. What is the main role of an activation function?
2. How is an activation function similar to a biological neuron firing?
3. Why are activation functions important for neural networks?
4. What does nonlinearity allow AI systems to do?
5. What range of values does the Sigmoid function produce?
6. Why is ReLU commonly used in modern AI systems?
7. What is the purpose of the Softmax function?
8. What happens if a neural network has no activation functions?
9. How do activation functions affect learning?
10. Why are activation functions called the "heartbeat" of AI?

Chapter 5 Worksheet

Part A: Understanding the Concept

1. In your own words, explain what an activation function does.

2. Name two activation functions and describe their purpose.

Part B: Thinking About Decisions

3. How does an activation function help a neuron decide what information is important?
4. Why is ignoring unimportant signals helpful for learning?

Part C: Reflection

5. Compare how humans decide what information to pay attention to with how artificial neurons activate.
6. Why is it useful for students to understand how AI makes decisions?

Chapter 5 Answer Key

Quiz Answers

1. It decides whether a neuron activates or stays inactive
2. Both activate only when a signal reaches a certain threshold
3. They allow networks to learn complex patterns
4. Handle real-world data that is not simple or straight-line
5. Between 0 and 1
6. It is simple, fast, and helps deep networks learn efficiently
7. To assign probabilities and make clear classifications
8. The network would be limited and unable to learn complex tasks
9. They guide which signals influence learning
10. Because they drive decision-making in neural networks

Worksheet Sample Answers

(Answers may vary)

1. It helps a neuron decide whether to pass information forward.
2. Sigmoid shows probability; ReLU focuses on positive signals.
3. It filters signals based on importance.
4. It prevents noise from affecting learning.
5. Both choose what matters and ignore what doesn't.
6. It helps students understand AI behavior and limitations.

Chapter 6: Backpropagation — Learning Through Mistakes

Every learner, whether human or machine, improves by recognizing errors and making adjustments. In education, when a student answers a question incorrectly, the teacher provides feedback, and the student learns what went wrong. This cycle of **trial, error, and correction** is at the heart of intelligence. Artificial neural networks operate on the same principle — a mathematical process called **backpropagation**, which literally means "propagating backward." It allows machines to learn from their mistakes and become smarter with every round of training.

WHAT IS BACKPROPAGATION?

Backpropagation is the process that allows artificial intelligence to learn from its mistakes. When a neural network makes a prediction, it checks how close that prediction is to the correct answer. If the result is wrong, the system does not stop — it learns from that mistake.

The word "backpropagation" means sending information backward. After the system produces an output, it sends the error back through the network to understand what went wrong. This allows the system to make small adjustments so it can perform better next time.

In simple terms, backpropagation is how machines improve. It turns mistakes into learning opportunities, helping the system become more accurate over time.

Backpropagation is one of the most important breakthroughs in the history of artificial intelligence. It gave neural networks the ability to refine their knowledge automatically, making modern deep learning possible. To understand how it works, let's imagine the network as a system of digital neurons, each with adjustable settings called **weights**. When data enters the network, it flows forward through the layers, producing an output — a prediction or decision. The machine then compares its output to the correct answer and measures how far off it is. This difference between the prediction and the truth is called the **error**.

UNDERSTANDING ERROR IN AI

Error in artificial intelligence is the difference between what the machine predicted and what the correct answer actually is. This difference shows how far the system is from being accurate.

For example, if a system predicts that an image is a dog but the correct answer is a cat, that difference is the error. The larger the error, the more the system needs to adjust its understanding.

Error is not a bad thing — it is a necessary part of learning. Without error, the system would have no way to improve. By measuring error, AI systems can identify where they went wrong and take steps to correct it.

The goal of backpropagation is to reduce this error over time. It does so by tracing the error backward through the network, identifying which neurons contributed most to the mistake. Once identified, the system adjusts the weights of those neurons slightly so they will perform better the next time. This process is repeated again and again with new data until the network becomes more accurate. Each correction may seem small, but over millions of iterations, these adjustments accumulate into true learning.

HOW NETWORKS CORRECT MISTAKES

Neural networks correct mistakes by adjusting values called weights. These weights control how important each piece of information is when making a decision.

When a mistake occurs, the system uses the error to determine which parts of the network contributed most to the problem. It then slightly adjusts the weights of those neurons to improve the next prediction.

These changes are usually very small, but they happen many times. With each adjustment, the network becomes a little more accurate. Over time, these small improvements add up, turning incorrect predictions into correct ones.

This process shows that learning is gradual. Just like humans improve through practice, machines improve through repeated correction.

GRADIENT DESCENT EXPLAINED

Gradient descent is the method that helps a neural network reduce its errors step by step. It works by guiding the system toward better and more accurate results.

A simple way to understand gradient descent is to imagine walking down a hill. Your goal is to reach the lowest point, which represents the smallest possible error. To get there, you take small steps downward, adjusting your direction as you go.

In AI, the system calculates the direction it needs to move to reduce the error. It then adjusts its weights slightly in that direction. If the steps are too large, it might miss the best solution. If the steps are too small, learning will be slow.

Gradient descent ensures that the system improves in a steady and controlled way, helping it reach the best possible performance over time.

At the core of backpropagation is a mathematical tool called **gradient descent**. Think of it like walking down a hill to reach the lowest point — the place of minimal error. The network calculates the slope, or "gradient," of the error function and takes small steps downhill, adjusting its weights along the way. If it takes steps that are too large, it might miss the bottom; if the steps are too small, learning will take too long. Finding the right balance ensures that the network learns efficiently and effectively.

This process of continuous feedback makes neural networks **adaptive systems**. They are not static programs that follow a fixed set of rules — they evolve. With every new example, the machine refines its understanding of the world. Just as a student learns to write better essays after reviewing feedback, a neural network learns to make more accurate predictions after backpropagation fine-tunes its parameters.

LEARNING THROUGH FEEDBACK

Feedback is an essential part of learning for both humans and machines. When a neural network receives feedback about its performance, it uses that information to improve.

In AI systems, feedback comes in the form of error. The system compares its prediction to the correct answer and uses that difference to guide future adjustments. This continuous cycle of prediction, feedback, and correction allows the system to grow more accurate.

Humans learn in a similar way. When students receive feedback on a test or assignment, they use it to improve their understanding. Machines follow the same pattern, using feedback to refine their internal processes.

This shows that learning is not about being perfect the first time — it is about improving over time through feedback.

One of the most powerful aspects of backpropagation is its **universality**. It can be applied to almost any kind of neural network — from those that recognize faces to those that drive cars or translate languages. Every time a model improves its accuracy, it is because backpropagation has quietly worked behind the scenes, correcting errors and reinforcing successful patterns. It is the invisible teacher of artificial intelligence.

To visualize this concept in the classroom, teachers might draw an analogy to a student studying for an exam. The "forward pass" is when the student answers the questions; the "error" is the score they receive. Backpropagation represents the student's review session — studying what went wrong, re-evaluating notes, and preparing to perform better next time. This makes the idea accessible and relatable, even to students new to AI.

CHALLENGES IN LEARNING

Although backpropagation is powerful, it is not always easy for neural networks to learn. One common challenge is known as the vanishing gradient problem.

In very deep networks, the error signal can become weaker as it moves backward through the layers. When this happens, the earlier layers do not receive enough information to improve, which slows down learning.

Researchers have developed techniques to solve this problem, such as better activation functions and improved network designs. These solutions help ensure that learning remains effective, even in complex systems.

Understanding these challenges helps students see that artificial intelligence is still evolving and improving.

However, backpropagation is not without its challenges. When networks become extremely deep, the flow of error signals can become weak — a problem known as the **vanishing gradient**. This can slow down or even halt learning. Researchers continue to develop new techniques, such as normalization and advanced activation functions, to overcome these obstacles. These innovations ensure that neural networks remain powerful tools capable of tackling increasingly complex problems.

WHY BACKPROPAGATION MATTERS

Backpropagation is one of the most important processes in artificial intelligence because it makes learning possible. Without it, neural networks would not be able to improve or adapt.

This process allows machines to learn from experience, just like humans do. It enables systems to recognize patterns, make better decisions, and become more accurate over time.

Backpropagation is used in many real-world applications, including image recognition, speech processing, and language translation. Every time an AI system improves its performance, backpropagation is working behind the scenes.

Understanding this process helps students see that intelligence is not about being perfect — it is about learning, adjusting, and growing over time.

Ultimately, backpropagation is a story of persistence — the same principle that drives human learning. It reminds us that intelligence, whether biological or artificial, grows through failure, reflection, and correction. Machines that learn through backpropagation are not just executing commands; they are engaging in an iterative dialogue with data — learning, improving, and approaching mastery with every cycle.

In the next chapter, we will explore the next great leap in artificial intelligence: **Deep Neural Networks and Deep Learning** — where many layers of artificial neurons work together to create machines capable of perception, reasoning, and creativity.

Chapter 6 Reflection

This chapter helps students understand that mistakes are not failures but opportunities to learn. Backpropagation shows that artificial intelligence improves by recognizing errors and adjusting its behavior. Just like students grow smarter by reviewing what they got wrong, machines grow smarter by correcting their internal settings.

Students are encouraged to reflect on how feedback plays a role in their own learning. Whether studying for a test or practicing a skill, improvement happens when mistakes are identified and addressed. This reflection helps students see that learning—human or machine—is a process built on patience, persistence, and correction.

This chapter also reminds students that intelligence is not fixed. Both people and machines evolve through effort and feedback. Understanding backpropagation helps students appreciate the value of learning from mistakes rather than fearing them.

Chapter 6 Summary

Backpropagation is the process that allows artificial neural networks to learn from their mistakes. When a neural network makes a prediction, it compares that result to the correct answer and calculates an error. This error shows how far the prediction is from the truth. Backpropagation works by sending this error backward through the network to identify which neurons contributed most to the mistake.

Once those neurons are identified, the network adjusts their weights slightly to improve future predictions. This adjustment happens using a method called gradient descent, which helps the network move step by step toward smaller errors. Over time, repeated corrections allow the network to become more accurate and reliable.

Backpropagation turns neural networks into adaptive systems that improve with experience. It is used in many real-world applications, including image recognition, language translation, and autonomous vehicles. Although challenges such as vanishing gradients exist, ongoing improvements continue to strengthen this learning method. By understanding backpropagation, students can see how intelligence grows through feedback, correction, and continuous learning.

Chapter 6 Quiz

1. What does the word "backpropagation" mean?
2. Why is backpropagation important for neural networks?
3. What is the "error" in machine learning?
4. How does a neural network use error to improve?
5. What are weights, and why are they adjusted?
6. What is gradient descent in simple terms?
7. How is backpropagation similar to how students learn?

8. What happens when learning steps are too large or too small?
9. What is the vanishing gradient problem?
10. Why is backpropagation called the "invisible teacher" of AI?

Chapter 6 Worksheet

Part A: Understanding the Process

1. Describe backpropagation using your own words.
2. Explain what happens during the "forward pass" and the "backward pass."

Part B: Thinking About Learning

3. Why are mistakes necessary for learning in AI systems?
4. How does feedback help both humans and machines improve?

Part C: Reflection

5. Think about a time you learned from a mistake. How is that similar to backpropagation?
6. Why is patience important when training both students and machines?

Chapter 6 Answer Key

Quiz Answers

1. Sending error information backward through the network
2. It allows the network to learn from mistakes
3. The difference between a prediction and the correct answer
4. By adjusting weights to reduce future errors
5. Weights control how important inputs are, and they are adjusted to improve accuracy
6. A method for slowly reducing error by taking small steps
7. Both improve by reviewing mistakes and making corrections
8. Learning may become unstable or too slow
9. When error signals become too weak in deep networks
10. Because it provides constant feedback and correction

Worksheet Sample Answers

(Answers may vary)

1. Backpropagation helps a machine fix mistakes by adjusting its settings.
2. The forward pass makes a prediction; the backward pass corrects errors.
3. Mistakes show what needs to be improved.
4. Feedback guides better decisions in the future.
5. Both involve reviewing errors and trying again.

6. Learning takes time and gradual improvement.

Chapter 7: Deep Neural Networks and Deep Learning

The journey of artificial intelligence takes a giant leap forward with the discovery of **Deep Neural Networks (DNNs)** — powerful systems that allow machines to see, hear, speak, and even make complex decisions. These deep networks form the core of what we now call **Deep Learning**, a branch of AI that has transformed how technology understands and interacts with the world. From self-driving cars to voice assistants, deep learning has become the silent intelligence behind many of the tools we use every day.

A **Deep Neural Network** is an extension of the basic neural network, but with a key difference: it contains many layers between the input and output. Each layer adds more depth and abstraction, enabling the machine to learn from data in increasingly sophisticated ways. In a simple neural network, the system might only recognize basic features — like edges or colors in an image. But in a deep network, the early layers learn those simple details, while the deeper layers combine them to recognize complex patterns such as faces, objects, or spoken words.

To visualize this, imagine teaching a student to recognize animals. At first, the student notices simple features — fur, tails, or claws. As learning continues, the student begins to connect those features: fur and whiskers might mean a cat, while scales and fins might mean a fish. This gradual layering of understanding mirrors how deep neural networks learn. Each layer extracts deeper meaning from the information it receives, building intelligence from the ground up.

The structure of a deep neural network can include dozens, hundreds, or even thousands of layers. The data flows forward through these layers, each one transforming it slightly before passing it on. Early layers capture low-level features; middle layers detect patterns or shapes; and final layers interpret the data into recognizable forms, such as identifying an image, predicting a number, or generating text. This hierarchical design allows machines to understand complex data with remarkable accuracy.

What makes deep learning so revolutionary is its ability to **automatically learn features** without needing humans to manually program every detail. In traditional programming, engineers had to tell computers exactly what to look for. Deep learning changes that — the network learns to discover the best features on its own, guided by experience and feedback. This self-learning capability is why deep networks outperform older AI systems in areas like speech recognition, translation, and visual analysis.

Training a deep neural network requires a large amount of **data** and computing power. Each layer contains millions of parameters — weights and biases — that must be adjusted through backpropagation. This process allows the network to fine-tune itself, gradually improving its predictions. Modern technologies such as **GPUs (Graphics Processing Units)** and **TPUs (Tensor Processing Units)** have made it possible to train these networks faster, turning what once took months into hours. These hardware advancements are the engines behind today's AI revolution.

One of the most fascinating aspects of deep learning is its ability to **generalize** — to recognize new examples it has never seen before. A deep network trained on pictures of cats can often recognize a cat in a completely new image, even if the pose, lighting, or background is different. This mirrors the human brain's ability to identify familiar objects under changing conditions, showcasing the incredible adaptability of deep architectures.

However, deep neural networks also have challenges. They require vast amounts of data, and when trained on biased information, they can unintentionally inherit those biases. They also consume significant energy and computational resources, raising ethical and environmental concerns. Despite these challenges, their contribution to modern society is undeniable — deep learning drives innovations in medicine, education, transportation, and beyond.

Teachers can use this chapter to show students how the depth of learning leads to the depth of understanding — both in machines and in humans. The deeper the network, the more abstract the learning becomes, just like how students progress from basic facts to complex reasoning. By comparing deep networks to the human brain's layered learning, students gain insight into how intelligence grows through accumulation and refinement.

Deep Neural Networks represent a milestone in the evolution of artificial intelligence — systems that not only process information but also **understand context and meaning**. In the next chapter, we will explore the variety of these networks — from feedforward to convolutional, recurrent, and transformer models — and discover how each type gives machines a different way of perceiving and reasoning about the world.

Chapter 7 Reflection

This chapter helps students understand that intelligence can grow in layers. Deep Neural Networks show how machines move beyond simple pattern recognition to deeper understanding by stacking many learning layers together. Reflecting on this idea helps students see that learning is not instant—it develops gradually as knowledge builds on itself.

Students are encouraged to think about how their own learning becomes deeper over time. At first, they learn basic facts. Later, they connect ideas, analyze meaning, and apply knowledge in new ways. This reflection shows that both humans and machines develop intelligence through layered learning and experience.

This chapter also invites students to consider responsibility. Deep learning systems are powerful, but they depend on data, computing resources, and human choices. Understanding how deep networks work helps students become thoughtful users and future designers of intelligent technology.

Chapter 7 Summary

Deep Neural Networks (DNNs) are advanced AI systems made up of many layers of artificial neurons. These layers allow machines to learn complex patterns and make sense of data such as images, sounds, and language. Deep learning is the method that uses these deep networks to power modern AI applications like voice assistants, self-driving cars, and medical imaging systems.

Each layer in a deep neural network learns something different. Early layers detect simple features, such as edges or sounds. Middle layers combine those features into patterns, and deeper layers interpret them into meaningful concepts like objects, words, or ideas. This layered structure allows machines to build understanding step by step, similar to how humans learn.

Deep learning is especially powerful because it can automatically discover important features without being explicitly programmed. Training these networks requires large amounts of data and strong computing power, supported by technologies such as GPUs and TPUs. While deep learning brings challenges like energy use and bias, it represents a major milestone in artificial intelligence—showing how depth of learning leads to depth of understanding.

Chapter 7 Quiz

1. What is a Deep Neural Network (DNN)?
2. How is deep learning different from simple neural networks?
3. Why are multiple layers important in deep learning?
4. What do early layers in a deep network usually learn?
5. What do deeper layers in a network focus on?
6. Why is deep learning considered revolutionary?
7. What role does backpropagation play in deep learning?
8. Why is large amounts of data needed for deep networks?
9. What does it mean when a deep network can generalize?
10. Name one challenge associated with deep learning.

Chapter 7 Worksheet

Part A: Understanding the Structure

1. Explain how a deep neural network builds understanding layer by layer.
2. List two real-world technologies that use deep learning.

Part B: Thinking About Learning

3. Why does deep learning not require humans to program every detail?
4. How is layered learning in machines similar to how students learn in school?

Part C: Reflection

5. Why do you think deeper learning leads to better understanding?
6. How can understanding deep learning help students become responsible technology users?

Chapter 7 Answer Key

Quiz Answers

1. A neural network with many layers that learns complex patterns
2. It uses many layers to learn deeper and more abstract features
3. Layers allow learning to become more detailed and meaningful
4. Simple features like edges, shapes, or sounds
5. Complex patterns such as objects, speech, or meaning
6. Because it allows machines to learn features automatically
7. It adjusts weights to improve accuracy
8. Because learning complex patterns requires many examples
9. It can recognize new data it has never seen before
10. High energy use, large data needs, or bias

Worksheet Sample Answers

(Answers may vary)

1. Each layer learns more complex information than the previous one.
2. Voice assistants, self-driving cars, medical imaging, translation tools.
3. The network discovers features on its own through training.
4. Students start with basics and build toward deeper understanding.
5. Deeper learning connects ideas and reveals meaning.
6. It helps students understand AI limits, power, and responsibility.

Chapter 8: Types of Neural Networks — Feedforward, RNN, CNN, and Transformer

Artificial intelligence is built upon many different neural network designs, each created to solve specific types of problems. Just as human intelligence expresses itself in diverse ways — language, memory, vision, and reasoning — artificial intelligence uses specialized architectures to handle text, images, sound, and sequences of events. These designs are the **types of neural networks**, and among the most important are **Feedforward Networks, Recurrent Neural Networks (RNNs), Convolutional Neural Networks (CNNs),** and **Transformer Networks**. Together, they form the foundation of modern deep learning.

Feedforward Neural Networks — The Simplest Path of Learning

The **Feedforward Neural Network** is the original and simplest form of artificial neural network. Information flows in one direction — from input to output — without looping back. Think of it as a straight road: data enters, gets processed by hidden layers, and exits as a prediction or classification. These networks are excellent for basic recognition tasks, such as predicting housing prices or identifying handwritten digits.

Each neuron in a feedforward network passes information forward after applying weights and activation functions, just like layers of understanding in a classroom — each layer refines what it receives before passing it on. However, feedforward networks have a limitation: they lack memory. They cannot recall past information, which makes them less effective for tasks that depend on sequences or time, such as predicting the next word in a sentence or understanding speech.

Despite this limitation, feedforward networks serve as the **building blocks of deep learning**, forming the conceptual backbone of more advanced models. They teach students one of AI's most important lessons — that learning begins with structure and order.

Recurrent Neural Networks (RNNs) — The Memory Keepers

Unlike feedforward networks, **Recurrent Neural Networks** introduce the concept of *memory*. In an RNN, information not only moves forward but can also loop back into the network. This looping mechanism allows the system to remember previous inputs and use them to influence future decisions.

For example, when reading a sentence, the meaning of a word often depends on the words that came before it. RNNs are designed to capture this kind of sequential relationship. They are widely used in **speech recognition, text translation, and time-series forecasting**, where context matters.

However, traditional RNNs face a challenge known as the **vanishing gradient problem**, where older information fades over time as the network learns new patterns. To overcome this, advanced versions like **Long Short-Term Memory (LSTM)** networks and **Gated Recurrent Units (GRUs)** were developed. These versions manage memory more effectively, allowing the network to retain information over longer sequences — much like how humans remember key details while reading a story.

Convolutional Neural Networks (CNNs) — The Visionaries

If RNNs are experts in memory, then **Convolutional Neural Networks** are experts in vision. CNNs are designed to process visual data, such as images and videos, by mimicking how the human brain interprets what it sees.

A CNN works by scanning small sections of an image at a time, identifying edges, colors, and textures. These details are processed through *convolutional layers*, which act like filters that detect specific patterns. As the data passes through multiple layers, the network learns to recognize more complex shapes and objects — faces, animals, vehicles, and more.

For instance, the first layer might detect edges, the second might identify corners or curves, and deeper layers might recognize entire objects. This hierarchical learning process allows CNNs to see the world in increasing detail. CNNs power technologies like **facial recognition, medical imaging diagnostics, autonomous vehicles, and surveillance systems**.

For students, CNNs illustrate how machines can "see" — not through eyes, but through mathematics. It's a remarkable example of how pattern recognition and numerical representation come together to simulate perception.

Transformer Networks — The Masters of Language and Context

The most advanced type of neural network today is the **Transformer**, a design that revolutionized natural language processing (NLP). Transformers excel at understanding relationships between words and meanings in large texts. They form the backbone of AI models that can summarize books, translate languages, write essays, and hold conversations — including systems like ChatGPT.

What makes Transformers unique is their **attention mechanism**. Instead of processing information in strict order, they analyze all parts of a sentence at once, deciding which words are most important to one another. This allows them to capture long-range dependencies and context with incredible accuracy. For example, in the sentence *"The bird sang while it perched on the branch,"* the Transformer knows that "it" refers to "bird," even though several words separate them.

Transformers are built with layers of **encoders and decoders**, each refining language understanding at different levels. They have become the standard for cutting-edge AI research, powering large language models (LLMs), machine translation systems, and content-generation tools.

Bringing It All Together

Each of these neural networks plays a unique role in the grand ecosystem of artificial intelligence:

- Feedforward Networks **process information efficiently** in one direction.
- Recurrent Networks **remember the past** to predict the future.
- Convolutional Networks **see the world** and recognize visual patterns.
- Transformer Networks **understand language** and relationships between ideas.

Together, they demonstrate that intelligence comes in many forms — visual, sequential, logical, and contextual.

Teachers can use this chapter to compare different types of learning in humans and machines. Just as students develop different skills — memory, vision, reasoning, and communication —

neural networks specialize in similar areas. Understanding these types helps students appreciate the diversity of AI systems shaping the modern world.

In the next chapter, we will explore **The Math Behind Learning — Simplified**, where we translate the mathematical heart of neural networks into concepts that students can easily grasp, connecting formulas with real-world meaning.

Chapter 8 Reflection

This chapter helps students understand that there is no single way for machines to learn. Just as humans use different skills for reading, remembering, seeing, and reasoning, artificial intelligence uses different types of neural networks for different tasks. Reflecting on this idea helps students see that intelligence comes in many forms, both human and artificial.

Students are encouraged to think about how memory, vision, and language work in their own lives. When reading a sentence, recognizing a face, or remembering past events, the brain uses different processes. This reflection shows that AI systems are designed in a similar way, with each network architecture specializing in a specific type of learning.

This chapter also invites students to appreciate that advanced AI systems are built by combining many specialized networks. Understanding these differences helps students become more informed users of technology and prepares them to think critically about how AI systems operate in the real world.

Chapter 8 Summary

Artificial intelligence relies on different types of neural networks to solve different problems. Feedforward networks, Recurrent Neural Networks (RNNs), Convolutional Neural Networks (CNNs), and Transformer networks each play a unique role in modern AI systems. These architectures allow machines to process information efficiently, remember sequences, recognize images, and understand language.

Feedforward neural networks are the simplest type. They move information in one direction from input to output and are useful for basic prediction and classification tasks. However, they lack memory and cannot handle sequential information. Recurrent Neural Networks solve this problem by allowing information to loop back, giving machines memory and context. This makes RNNs useful for tasks like speech recognition and language translation, though advanced versions such as LSTMs and GRUs are often used to improve long-term memory.

Convolutional Neural Networks are designed for visual understanding. By scanning images in small sections, CNNs learn to recognize edges, shapes, and objects, powering technologies like facial recognition and medical imaging. Transformer networks represent the most advanced architecture, using attention mechanisms to understand language and context across large amounts of text. Together, these neural networks show that intelligence is specialized, layered, and adaptable—just like human learning.

Chapter 8 Quiz

1. Why do AI systems use different types of neural networks?
2. What is the main feature of a feedforward neural network?
3. Why are feedforward networks limited for language tasks?
4. What makes Recurrent Neural Networks different from feedforward networks?
5. What problem do LSTMs and GRUs help solve?
6. What type of data are Convolutional Neural Networks best at processing?
7. How do CNNs learn to recognize objects in images?
8. What makes Transformer networks unique?
9. What is an attention mechanism used for?
10. How do different neural networks work together in modern AI systems?

Chapter 8 Worksheet

Part A: Matching Networks to Tasks

1. Match each neural network type to its main strength:
   - Feedforward
   - RNN
   - CNN
   - Transformer
2. Give one real-world example for each type of neural network.

Part B: Understanding Differences

3. Explain why memory is important for understanding language.
4. Why is vision processing different from text processing in AI?

Part C: Reflection

5. Which neural network type do you think is most impressive, and why?
6. How does understanding different AI models help students use technology more responsibly?

Chapter 8 Answer Key

Quiz Answers

1. Different problems require different learning structures
2. Information flows in one direction only
3. They cannot remember past information
4. They include memory through looping connections
5. The vanishing gradient problem
6. Images and visual data

7. By detecting patterns like edges, shapes, and objects
8. They use attention to understand context across text
9. To determine which words or information are most important
10. They handle different tasks such as vision, memory, and language

Worksheet Sample Answers

(Answers may vary)

1.

- Feedforward → Simple prediction
- RNN → Memory and sequences
- CNN → Vision and images
- Transformer → Language and context

2.

- Feedforward: price prediction
- RNN: speech recognition
- CNN: facial recognition
- Transformer: language translation

3. Memory helps machines understand meaning across sentences.
4. Images rely on spatial patterns, while text relies on sequence and context.
5. Answers may vary based on interest.
6. It helps students understand AI strengths, limits, and ethical use.

Chapter 9: The Math Behind Learning — Simplified

Artificial intelligence may seem magical, but at its core, it is powered by **mathematics** — the language of logic and precision. Just as letters form the foundation of written language, math forms the foundation of machine intelligence. Every prediction, every pattern, and every decision a neural network makes can be traced back to numbers, equations, and relationships between them. Understanding these mathematical roots helps students see that intelligence, both human and artificial, is built upon patterns that can be measured, analyzed, and understood.

At the heart of this mathematical foundation lies a simple idea: **machines learn by adjusting numbers.** These numbers are called **weights and biases**, and they control how strongly one neuron influences another. During training, the network changes these values little by little until the outputs become accurate. This process is guided by the same principles students use when solving problems — guessing, checking, and correcting. Mathematics gives structure to that learning, allowing the machine to move closer to the right answer each time.

One of the most important operations in neural networks is **multiplication**, followed by **addition**. When data passes into the network, each input is multiplied by its corresponding weight. Then, all the weighted inputs are added together, and a bias is applied. The result of this equation is then passed through an activation function to determine whether the neuron "fires." In symbolic form, it can be written as:

Output = Activation (Weight × Input + Bias).

Though this may seem complex, it's actually the mathematical version of a simple idea: deciding what matters most.

To illustrate this in human terms, imagine grading homework. Each question has a certain importance (weight). You multiply each student's score by that weight and add them all together to get a final grade. Similarly, the neural network calculates how important each piece of input data is and makes its decision based on those combined results. Mathematics helps the machine judge the "importance" of data points, giving structure to its intelligence.

Another crucial concept in AI mathematics is **functions**. A function takes an input, performs a specific operation, and gives an output. In machine learning, functions describe how data transforms as it moves through the network. Linear functions handle simple, straight-line relationships. Nonlinear functions handle more complex curves, allowing machines to learn intricate relationships in the data — such as how words relate in language or how shapes combine in an image. Nonlinear equations make learning flexible and realistic, mirroring the complexities of life.

Then comes **optimization**, the mathematical process of improvement. Using equations, the machine finds the best combination of weights and biases to minimize errors. This is where calculus — specifically **derivatives and gradients** — comes into play. The gradient tells the machine the direction and size of change needed to improve its accuracy. When used in algorithms like **gradient descent**, the system takes small mathematical steps toward better performance. It's like climbing down a mountain of errors until it reaches the lowest point — the optimal solution.

Statistics also play a vital role in teaching machines how to learn. Through **probability**, AI systems handle uncertainty and make predictions. For instance, a model might predict that there's an 85% chance a given image shows a cat. It doesn't claim absolute certainty — it calculates likelihoods based on patterns learned from past examples. This probabilistic reasoning allows AI to make sound judgments even when data is imperfect or incomplete.

Teachers can use this chapter to connect mathematics with real-world problem-solving. Students who once wondered, "When will I ever use math?" will see that algebra, geometry, and calculus form the backbone of modern technology. From search engines to streaming recommendations, all of them rely on equations running silently in the background. Understanding this bridge between math and intelligence helps students see learning as a creative process — not just numbers on paper, but a living system of reasoning.

In the end, mathematics is the **engine of intelligence**. It gives order to randomness, direction to learning, and structure to thought. Machines may not feel or dream, but through equations, they learn, adapt, and reason in a way that reflects the mathematical harmony of the universe.

In the next chapter, we will explore **Neural Network Architectures in the Real World** — discovering how all these mathematical principles come together to power the smart systems that shape our modern lives.

Chapter 9 Reflection

This chapter helps students understand that artificial intelligence is not magic — it is built on mathematics. Every decision a machine makes comes from numbers working together in structured ways. Reflecting on this idea helps students realize that math is not just a school subject, but a tool that shapes the intelligent systems they interact with every day.

Students are encouraged to think about how math helps both humans and machines learn. Just as students solve problems by testing ideas and correcting mistakes, AI systems adjust numbers to improve accuracy. This reflection shows that learning, whether human or artificial, is guided by logic, structure, and patience.

The chapter also invites students to see math as creative rather than intimidating. Mathematics gives machines the ability to reason, adapt, and make predictions. Understanding this helps students feel more confident about both AI and their own problem-solving abilities.

Chapter 9 Summary

Artificial intelligence is powered by mathematics, which provides the structure behind learning, reasoning, and decision-making. Neural networks rely on numbers called weights and biases to determine how strongly information influences outcomes. During training, these values are adjusted little by little until the system becomes more accurate. This process mirrors how humans learn by testing ideas and refining their thinking.

At the center of neural network math is a simple equation: inputs are multiplied by weights, combined with a bias, and passed through an activation function. This calculation helps the machine decide what information matters most. Functions play an important role in this process, allowing data to change as it moves through the network. Linear functions handle simple relationships, while nonlinear functions allow machines to learn complex patterns found in language, images, and real-world situations.

Optimization techniques such as gradient descent help machines reduce errors by moving step by step toward better solutions. Probability and statistics allow AI systems to handle uncertainty and make predictions based on likelihood rather than absolute certainty. Together, these mathematical tools form the engine of machine learning. Understanding this foundation helps students see how math connects directly to modern technology and why mathematical thinking is essential in the intelligent age.

Chapter 9 Quiz

1. What is the role of mathematics in artificial intelligence?
2. What are weights and biases in a neural network?
3. Why do machines adjust numbers during learning?
4. What does the equation
   Output = Activation (Weight × Input + Bias) represent?
5. How is grading homework similar to how neural networks work?
6. Why are functions important in machine learning?
7. What is the purpose of nonlinear functions?
8. What does optimization help AI systems do?
9. How does probability help AI make decisions?
10. Why is math described as the "engine" of intelligence?

Chapter 9 Worksheet

Part A: Understanding the Basics

1. Explain in your own words how math helps machines learn.
2. Name two mathematical concepts used in AI and describe their role.

Part B: Thinking About Learning

3. Why is adjusting weights and biases important for improving accuracy?
4. How does gradient descent help reduce errors?

Part C: Reflection

5. How does learning math help you better understand AI systems?
6. Why is it important for students to see math as useful in real life?

Chapter 9 Answer Key

Quiz Answers

1. Math provides the structure for learning and decision-making
2. Numbers that control how strongly inputs affect outputs
3. To improve accuracy and reduce errors
4. How a neuron processes information and makes a decision
5. Both weigh importance and combine results to reach an outcome
6. They describe how data is transformed
7. They allow learning of complex relationships
8. It helps find the best values to minimize errors
9. It allows predictions based on likelihood
10. Because it drives learning, reasoning, and structure

Worksheet Sample Answers

(Answers may vary)

1. Math allows machines to adjust numbers to learn patterns.
2. Weights control importance; functions transform data.
3. Adjusting them helps the machine make better predictions.
4. It moves the system toward smaller errors step by step.
5. It helps students understand how AI decisions are made.
6. It shows that math powers real-world technology.

Chapter 10: Neural Network Architectures in the Real World

Artificial Neural Networks are not just theoretical models — they are the engines driving much of modern technology. From the moment you unlock your smartphone with facial recognition to the instant your favorite app suggests a song or a product, **neural network architectures** are working behind the scenes. Each type of architecture is designed to solve a specific class of problems. The real-world applications of these networks reveal how data, numbers, and neurons come together to create practical intelligence.

A **neural network architecture** refers to the overall structure and design of how neurons are organized and connected within a system. Just as architects design buildings with specific functions — schools, hospitals, bridges — engineers design neural networks to perform specific tasks. Some architectures excel at recognizing images, while others are built for understanding language, detecting sound, or making decisions over time. The beauty of this design lies in its versatility — a single concept, inspired by the brain, can be reshaped to fit countless purposes.

One of the most common architectures in real-world use is the **Convolutional Neural Network (CNN)**, which has revolutionized how machines "see." CNNs are behind image classification, object detection, and facial recognition. For example, when you upload a photo to your social media account and it automatically tags your friends, a CNN is identifying their faces by analyzing patterns of pixels. In healthcare, CNNs are used to detect tumors and anomalies in medical scans, sometimes identifying issues that even trained professionals might miss. These systems show how neural networks extend human perception into new realms of precision.

Another influential architecture is the **Recurrent Neural Network (RNN)**, which powers systems that understand sequences and time-based data. RNNs are used in applications like speech recognition, translation, and financial forecasting. For instance, when you dictate a message and your device types it accurately, an RNN is analyzing your voice patterns in real time, predicting each word based on what you've already said. These networks function like memory keepers — they remember context, making them ideal for language and sequential decision-making.

The next evolution in neural network design is the **Transformer architecture**, which has reshaped how AI understands and generates human language. Transformers use a mechanism called **attention**, allowing them to process all parts of a sentence simultaneously and determine which words are most important to each other. This architecture powers large language models that can translate text, summarize information, write essays, or answer complex questions — like the one you are reading now. Transformers represent the peak of linguistic intelligence in machines, transforming how people learn, create, and communicate.

Other architectures are designed for **decision-making and interaction**. For example, **Deep Reinforcement Learning Networks** are used in robotics and gaming. These systems learn through rewards and feedback, much like humans do. When a robot learns to walk or a computer program learns to play chess better than a grandmaster, it's because these networks have practiced through thousands of simulated experiences, improving with each step. These architectures teach machines how to explore, adapt, and respond dynamically to their environments.

In the real world, neural networks rarely exist in isolation. They are often **combined and layered**, forming hybrid architectures that work together to solve multifaceted problems. For instance, a self-driving car might use CNNs to interpret camera images, RNNs to predict the movement of other vehicles, and reinforcement learning models to make safe driving decisions. Each component plays a role — like organs in a living body — working together to create intelligent, coordinated behavior.

Teachers can use this chapter to connect theory to practice. Students can research examples of neural networks in daily life — from voice assistants and smart thermostats to spam filters and personalized learning apps. By understanding these systems, students begin to see artificial intelligence not as an abstract idea but as a tangible part of the world they live in. The goal is to help them recognize that behind every "smart" technology is a carefully designed network of artificial neurons working tirelessly to interpret, learn, and improve.

In the real world, neural networks are quietly transforming how industries operate. In education, they personalize learning. In healthcare, they diagnose diseases. In transportation, they guide vehicles safely. In entertainment, they recommend music and movies. What began as a theoretical model inspired by the human brain has become a universal framework for innovation — one that touches every aspect of modern life.

In the next chapter, we will uncover the **hardware** that powers these digital brains — the GPUs, TPUs, and chips that form the physical foundation of artificial intelligence.

Chapter 10 Reflection

This chapter helps students realize that artificial intelligence is not just something studied in books — it is active in the real world every day. Neural network architectures are the hidden systems behind many technologies students already use, such as smartphones, streaming platforms, and voice assistants. Reflecting on this idea helps students see AI as practical and real, not distant or abstract.

Students are encouraged to think about how different problems require different solutions. Just as humans use different skills for seeing, remembering, and decision-making, AI systems use different neural network architectures for different tasks. This reflection highlights that intelligence is flexible and specialized.

The chapter also invites students to consider responsibility. Because neural networks influence important areas like healthcare, education, and transportation, understanding how they work helps students become informed, thoughtful users of intelligent technology.

Chapter 10 Summary

Neural network architectures are the structured designs that allow artificial intelligence systems to solve real-world problems. Each architecture is built with a specific purpose, just as buildings are designed for different uses. These architectures organize artificial neurons in ways that allow machines to see images, understand language, remember sequences, and make decisions.

Convolutional Neural Networks (CNNs) are widely used for visual tasks such as facial recognition, medical imaging, and object detection. Recurrent Neural Networks (RNNs) specialize in understanding sequences and time-based data, making them useful for speech recognition, translation, and forecasting. Transformer networks represent a major advancement in language understanding, using attention mechanisms to analyze context and relationships across large pieces of text.

Other architectures, such as deep reinforcement learning networks, help machines learn through rewards and feedback, powering robotics and advanced game-playing systems. In real-world applications, these networks are often combined into hybrid systems. For example, self-driving cars use multiple architectures together to see, predict, and act safely. Understanding these architectures helps students see how artificial intelligence moves from theory to practical intelligence that shapes modern life.

Chapter 10 Quiz

1. What is a neural network architecture?
2. Why are different architectures used for different tasks?
3. What real-world tasks are Convolutional Neural Networks best at?
4. How do Recurrent Neural Networks help machines understand information?
5. What makes Transformer networks different from earlier models?
6. What role does attention play in Transformers?
7. How do reinforcement learning networks learn?
8. Why are neural networks often combined in real-world systems?
9. Give one example of AI used in everyday life.
10. Why is it important for students to understand real-world AI systems?

Chapter 10 Worksheet

Part A: Connecting Architecture to Application

1. Match each neural network architecture to its main use:
   - CNN
   - RNN
   - Transformer
   - Reinforcement Learning Network
2. Describe one real-world example where neural networks are used.

Part B: Thinking Critically

3. Why would a self-driving car need more than one type of neural network?
4. How does combining networks improve AI performance?

Part C: Reflection

5. How does learning about neural networks change how you view everyday technology?
6. Why is it important for students to think about ethics and responsibility when using AI?

Chapter 10 Answer Key

Quiz Answers

1. The design and structure of how neurons are connected in a network
2. Different problems require different learning methods
3. Image recognition, facial detection, and medical imaging
4. By remembering past information and context
5. They process all parts of text at once using attention
6. It helps the model focus on important relationships
7. Through rewards and feedback
8. To solve complex problems more effectively
9. Voice assistants, recommendations, facial recognition, or navigation
10. To understand how AI affects society and decision-making

Worksheet Sample Answers

(Answers may vary)

1.

- CNN → Vision and images
- RNN → Sequences and memory
- Transformer → Language and context
- Reinforcement Learning → Decision-making

2. Facial recognition on smartphones.
3. It must see the road, predict movement, and make decisions.
4. Each network handles a different part of the problem.

5. It helps students realize AI is everywhere.
6. AI decisions can affect people's lives.

Chapter 11: Hardware of the Brain — GPUs, TPUs, and Chips

Every intelligent system needs a brain — a place where thinking, processing, and learning occur. In humans, that brain is made of billions of biological neurons powered by electrical and chemical signals. In machines, the brain exists within **hardware** — the physical components that make computation possible. These are the **processors, chips, and specialized units** that bring artificial intelligence to life. Just as neurons in the human brain fire rapidly to process information, these electronic components perform billions of calculations every second, enabling machines to see, hear, and reason.

The foundation of all AI hardware lies in the **Central Processing Unit (CPU)**, the general-purpose processor found in every computer. The CPU is excellent at handling a wide range of tasks — from running software to managing files — but it struggles when asked to process the enormous quantities of data required for modern AI. That's where more advanced and specialized hardware enters the scene: **Graphics Processing Units (GPUs)**, **Tensor Processing Units (TPUs)**, and custom **AI chips** designed for deep learning.

GPUs — The Workhorses of AI

Originally designed to render images and graphics in video games, **GPUs** have become the backbone of deep learning. A GPU contains thousands of smaller cores that can perform many calculations simultaneously — a process known as **parallel computing**. While a CPU might handle a few complex tasks at a time, a GPU can handle thousands of smaller ones all at once, making it ideal for training neural networks that rely on large-scale matrix operations.

When a neural network learns, it must multiply millions of numbers repeatedly — a task that fits perfectly with the GPU's parallel architecture. Companies like **NVIDIA** and **AMD** have spent years optimizing GPUs for AI workloads, transforming them from gaming tools into powerful engines of machine intelligence. Every major AI model today — from computer vision systems to language models — depends on GPUs to think and learn efficiently.

TPUs — The Specialized Thinkers

While GPUs revolutionized AI training, **Tensor Processing Units (TPUs)** took it a step further. Developed by **Google**, TPUs are custom-designed processors built specifically for machine learning tasks. The word "tensor" comes from TensorFlow, Google's popular AI framework, and refers to the multi-dimensional data arrays that neural networks use.

TPUs excel at performing tensor operations quickly and efficiently. They are optimized for both **training** and **inference** — meaning they can teach AI models as well as deploy them in real-world applications. TPUs consume less power than GPUs while achieving faster results, making them an essential component of Google's vast AI infrastructure. When you use services like Google Translate or Google Photos, TPUs are quietly at work behind the scenes, processing data at lightning speed.

AI Chips — The Custom Brains of the Future

Beyond GPUs and TPUs, a new generation of hardware has emerged: **AI chips**. These are specialized processors built by companies like **NVIDIA, Intel, Apple, Tesla, and Meta** to handle specific AI functions. Each chip is designed to accelerate machine learning tasks while reducing power consumption.

For instance, **NVIDIA's A100 and H100 chips** are used in data centers around the world to train massive language models and complex neural networks. **Apple's Neural Engine**, integrated into iPhones and iPads, processes AI tasks locally — enabling features like face recognition, voice assistance, and photo enhancement without sending data to the cloud. **Tesla's Dojo chip** powers the company's self-driving technology, processing video data from cars in real time. Each of these chips represents a new form of synthetic cognition, giving machines the raw power to think faster and smarter.

The Marriage of Hardware and Intelligence

The success of AI depends not only on algorithms but also on the physical strength of its hardware. Just as a human brain needs healthy neurons to function, an AI system needs powerful processors to execute its calculations. Hardware enables speed, and speed enables learning. Without it, even the most advanced algorithms would remain theoretical ideas — too slow to be useful.

This is why global industries invest heavily in hardware innovation. The world's largest technology companies compete to design faster, smaller, and more energy-efficient chips. Cloud providers like Amazon Web Services, Microsoft Azure, and Google Cloud rent out GPU and TPU clusters, allowing researchers, students, and companies to train AI models from anywhere in the world. These systems form the **digital nervous system of modern civilization**.

For the Classroom

Teachers can use this chapter to help students visualize how intelligence moves from software to hardware. Just as biology classes teach how the human brain's anatomy supports its function, this chapter reveals how AI's "electronic brain" operates. Students can explore images of GPUs and chips, learn about parallel processing, and even research which devices in their homes already use AI-powered hardware.

Ultimately, GPUs, TPUs, and AI chips represent the **heartbeat of artificial intelligence** — the silent machinery that transforms lines of code into living, thinking systems. They remind us that behind every act of machine intelligence lies an intricate dance of electrons, circuits, and logic — all working together to mimic the power of thought.

In the next chapter, we will explore another essential ingredient of learning: **Training Data and Bias**, and how the information we give to machines can shape the fairness, accuracy, and ethics of their intelligence.

Chapter 11 Reflection

This chapter helps students understand that artificial intelligence does not exist only in software. Machines need physical hardware to think, learn, and make decisions. GPUs, TPUs, and AI chips act as the electronic brains that allow AI systems to process enormous amounts of data quickly.

Students are encouraged to reflect on how hardware affects learning. Just as the human brain relies on healthy neurons to think clearly, AI systems rely on powerful processors to learn efficiently. Without advanced hardware, even the best algorithms would be too slow to be useful.

This chapter also invites students to recognize how close AI hardware is to everyday life. Many devices they already use—phones, tablets, cars, and online services—contain specialized chips that make intelligent features possible. Understanding this helps students see AI as a real, physical system shaping the modern world.

Chapter 11 Summary

Artificial intelligence depends on hardware—the physical components that perform calculations and make learning possible. While the CPU serves as the general-purpose processor in computers, modern AI requires more powerful and specialized hardware to handle massive amounts of data. This need led to the development of GPUs, TPUs, and custom AI chips.

GPUs are the workhorses of AI. Their ability to perform thousands of calculations at the same time makes them ideal for training neural networks. GPUs transformed AI research by allowing models to learn faster and more efficiently. TPUs, developed by Google, are even more specialized. They are designed specifically for machine learning tasks, performing tensor operations quickly while using less energy. TPUs power many large-scale AI services used every day.

AI chips represent the future of machine intelligence. Companies design custom processors to handle specific AI tasks with greater speed and efficiency. From data centers training massive models to smartphones running AI locally, these chips form the physical foundation of artificial intelligence. Together, AI hardware and algorithms create systems capable of learning, reasoning, and transforming modern society.

Chapter 11 Quiz

1. Why is hardware important for artificial intelligence?

2. What role does the CPU play in a computer system?
3. Why are CPUs not ideal for modern AI tasks?
4. What makes GPUs powerful for AI learning?
5. What is parallel computing?
6. What are TPUs designed to do?
7. Why are TPUs more energy-efficient than GPUs?
8. What are AI chips, and why are they important?
9. Give one example of AI hardware used in everyday devices.
10. Why is AI hardware compared to the brain of a machine?

Chapter 11 Worksheet

Part A: Understanding AI Hardware

1. Explain the difference between a CPU and a GPU in your own words.
2. Name two tasks that GPUs are especially good at handling.

Part B: Thinking About Technology

3. Why do AI systems need specialized hardware instead of general processors?
4. How does faster hardware help AI learn more effectively?

Part C: Reflection

5. List two devices in your home that may use AI hardware.
6. Why is it important for students to understand how AI hardware works?

Chapter 11 Answer Key

Quiz Answers

1. Hardware allows AI to process data and learn quickly
2. It handles general computer tasks and instructions
3. They are too slow for large-scale AI calculations
4. They can perform many calculations at the same time
5. Doing many calculations simultaneously
6. To perform machine learning tasks efficiently
7. They are optimized specifically for AI operations
8. Specialized processors designed for AI tasks
9. Smartphones, cars, or cloud services
10. Because it enables thinking, learning, and decision-making

Worksheet Sample Answers

(Answers may vary)

1. A CPU handles general tasks, while a GPU handles many calculations at once.
2. Training neural networks and processing images.
3. Specialized hardware is faster and more efficient.
4. It allows models to train and improve quickly.
5. Smartphones, smart TVs, or voice assistants.
6. It helps students understand how AI works in real life.

Chapter 12: Training Data and Bias

Every intelligent machine begins its journey as a learner — eager to recognize patterns, make predictions, and understand the world. But the quality of what it learns depends entirely on the **data** it receives. This is called **training data**, and it serves as the foundation upon which artificial intelligence builds its knowledge. Just as a child learns by observing examples, a neural network learns by studying the data it is given. However, if those examples are incomplete, unfair, or unbalanced, the machine's understanding will also be flawed. This is where the concept of **bias** becomes critically important.

The Role of Training Data

Training data is the collection of examples that teaches a machine what to do. For a system that recognizes animals, the training data might include thousands of labeled images of cats, dogs, and birds. For a translation model, it might include millions of sentences written in different languages. Each piece of data helps the system build a mental map — a representation of the world it's trying to understand.

The process of training involves feeding this data into the neural network repeatedly, allowing the model to find patterns and relationships. Over time, it becomes capable of making predictions about new, unseen data. In this way, training data functions as the teacher, and the AI system is the student. The quality, diversity, and balance of that data determine how well the student learns.

But not all data is equal. If a student learns from incomplete or biased textbooks, their understanding will be limited. The same is true for machines. If the training data lacks diversity or reflects human prejudices, the AI will inherit those same patterns. This leads to **algorithmic bias** — an invisible but powerful force that can distort how machines perceive and act.

Understanding Bias in AI

Bias in artificial intelligence occurs when a model's predictions or behaviors systematically favor or discriminate against certain groups, outcomes, or ideas. It's not always intentional; in fact, bias often creeps in quietly through the data itself. For example, if a hiring algorithm is trained mostly on résumés from men, it may unconsciously learn to favor male applicants. If a facial recognition system is trained mostly on light-skinned faces, it might perform poorly on darker skin tones. These biases are reflections of the imbalance present in the training data — not malicious design, but imperfect representation.

Bias can enter an AI system in several ways. It can come from **sampling bias** (when certain groups are underrepresented in the dataset), **labeling bias** (when human annotators make subjective judgments), or **historical bias** (when old data reflects outdated social inequalities). These biases can lead to unfair or inaccurate outcomes, particularly in sensitive areas like hiring, education, law enforcement, or healthcare.

Recognizing bias is the first step toward addressing it. Engineers and researchers now use **bias detection and mitigation techniques** to measure and reduce inequality in datasets. This may involve diversifying data sources, balancing representation, or using algorithms designed to correct unfair patterns. Teachers can use this concept to help students see how fairness and responsibility must guide every stage of technology development.

The Importance of Diversity and Quality

For an AI system to learn fairly and effectively, its training data must be **diverse, balanced, and accurate**. This means including examples from many cultures, languages, genders, and environments. When data reflects the true diversity of human experience, machines are better equipped to make fair and reliable decisions.

High-quality data also needs to be **clean** — free from errors, duplicates, and irrelevant information. Students can imagine this as organizing their notes before an exam: if the notes are messy or incomplete, understanding will suffer. In AI, clean and balanced data lead to trustworthy intelligence.

Ethics in Machine Learning

Ethical responsibility in AI begins with data collection. Engineers must ask important questions:

- Who created this data?
- Does it represent everyone fairly?
- Could it cause harm if used incorrectly?

These questions are not just technical; they are moral. Every dataset carries traces of human choices and values. When machines learn from us, they also learn about us — our priorities, our perspectives, and sometimes our prejudices. That's why ethics must be part of every AI project, from design to deployment.

Teachers can turn this into meaningful classroom discussions by comparing machine learning bias to real-world fairness. For example, students might analyze how biased information in media or history books can shape public opinion — then relate it to how biased data can shape AI behavior. These lessons build not only technological literacy but also digital citizenship.

The Shared Responsibility

AI bias is not just a problem for programmers — it's a shared human responsibility. Data scientists, educators, policymakers, and users must work together to ensure that artificial intelligence serves everyone equally. Creating fair AI systems means listening to diverse voices, testing models for inclusivity, and teaching future generations to value accuracy and empathy as much as efficiency.

When students understand how bias affects both humans and machines, they learn a vital lesson: intelligence must be guided by fairness. Machines can only mirror what we give them. If we provide them with truth, balance, and compassion, they will reflect those same qualities back to society.

Chapter 12 Reflection

This chapter helps students understand that artificial intelligence learns from examples, just like humans do. The data given to a machine shapes how it thinks, decides, and acts. Reflecting on this idea helps students realize that AI is not neutral by default — it reflects the information it is taught.

Students are encouraged to think about how unfair or incomplete information can lead to misunderstandings. Just as biased teaching materials can affect students, biased training data can affect machines. This reflection shows that learning is only as fair as the examples used to teach.

The chapter also invites students to see their role in shaping the future of AI. Because humans create and use data, they share responsibility for making sure AI systems are accurate, fair, and respectful of all people.

Chapter 12 Summary

Training data is the foundation of artificial intelligence learning. It is the collection of examples that teaches machines how to recognize patterns, make predictions, and understand the world. Neural networks study training data repeatedly, learning from it in much the same way students learn from textbooks and lessons. The quality, balance, and diversity of this data determine how well an AI system performs.

Bias occurs when training data is incomplete, unbalanced, or reflects human prejudice. This can cause AI systems to favor certain groups or make unfair decisions. Bias may come from missing data, subjective labeling, or historical inequalities reflected in older information. These problems often appear in sensitive areas such as hiring, education, healthcare, and public safety.

To reduce bias, AI systems must be trained on diverse, accurate, and carefully reviewed data. Ethical responsibility begins at data collection and continues through testing and deployment. Understanding training data and bias helps students see that intelligence must be guided by fairness and care. When machines learn from balanced and ethical data, they are more likely to serve society in responsible and trustworthy ways.

Chapter 12 Quiz

1. What is training data in artificial intelligence?
2. Why is training data compared to a teacher?
3. What does bias in AI mean?
4. How can biased data affect AI decisions?
5. Name one example of how bias can appear in AI systems.
6. What is sampling bias?
7. Why is diversity important in training data?
8. How does poor-quality data affect learning?
9. Why is ethics important in machine learning?
10. Who is responsible for reducing bias in AI systems?

Chapter 12 Worksheet

Part A: Understanding Key Ideas

1. Explain why training data is important for AI learning.
2. Describe bias using your own words.

Part B: Thinking Critically

3. What could happen if an AI system is trained on unbalanced data?
4. How can engineers and researchers reduce bias in AI systems?

Part C: Reflection

5. Give an example of how bias in information can affect human decisions.
6. Why is it important for students to understand fairness in AI?

Chapter 12 Answer Key

Quiz Answers

1. The examples used to teach an AI system
2. Because it teaches the machine how to learn and decide
3. Unfair or unbalanced behavior caused by flawed data
4. It can lead to unfair or inaccurate outcomes
5. Facial recognition working better for some groups than others
6. When some groups are underrepresented in data
7. It helps AI make fair and accurate decisions
8. It leads to confusion and unreliable results
9. AI decisions can affect people's lives
10. Everyone involved — designers, users, and society

Worksheet Sample Answers

(Answers may vary)

1. Training data teaches machines what patterns to learn.
2. Bias means unfair influence in learning or decision-making.
3. The AI may favor certain groups unfairly.
4. By using diverse data and checking results carefully.
5. Biased news or history books shaping opinions.
6. It helps students become responsible digital citizens.

Chapter 13: Data Visualization — Seeing the Story Behind Numbers

In the world of artificial intelligence and data science, information often begins as a collection of raw numbers — vast, complex, and difficult to interpret. Yet behind those numbers lie stories, patterns, and truths waiting to be discovered. The art and science of **data visualization** transforms those hidden insights into images that the human mind can easily understand. Just as artists use color and shape to express emotion, scientists use charts, graphs, and visual tools to reveal meaning. Data visualization is where mathematics meets creativity — a bridge between numbers and human understanding.

The Power of Seeing Data

Humans are visual learners. Our brains process images much faster than text or numbers. This natural ability makes visualization an essential part of both learning and discovery. When data is displayed visually, patterns that were once invisible suddenly become clear. For example, a line graph can show how temperatures change over time, while a bar chart can compare different categories of information. These visuals allow students and researchers to spot trends, outliers, and relationships at a glance — something that would be nearly impossible by looking at numbers alone.

In artificial intelligence, data visualization plays a critical role in **training, analyzing, and explaining models**. Engineers use visual tools to monitor how a machine learns, detect where it struggles, and understand how decisions are made. Teachers can draw a powerful classroom analogy: visualization is like a progress chart for a student — it helps show growth, identify weaknesses, and celebrate improvement.

Common Visualization Tools and Methods

There are many ways to visualize data, each suited to different types of information. Some of the most common include:

- **Bar Charts** – Compare quantities across categories (e.g., number of students per grade).
- **Line Graphs** – Show trends over time (e.g., monthly growth in website visitors).
- **Pie Charts** – Illustrate proportions (e.g., percentage of AI applications in various industries).
- **Scatter Plots** – Reveal relationships between variables (e.g., study hours vs. test scores).
- **Heat Maps** – Display data intensity or frequency using color (e.g., traffic activity across a city).

In AI and machine learning, specialized visualizations such as **confusion matrices, loss curves, and activation maps** help engineers see how well a neural network performs. These visual tools guide improvements, just as graphs in science experiments help students analyze results.

Turning Data into Insight

Visualization is not just about creating pretty charts — it's about uncovering meaning. When data is visualized thoughtfully, it becomes a **story** that can inform, persuade, and inspire. For example, a teacher showing how test scores improved after a new learning method isn't just presenting numbers; they're telling a story of growth. In the same way, an AI researcher visualizing data on climate change is revealing the story of our planet's transformation.

This process of storytelling through data helps bridge the gap between **technical information** and **human emotion**. Students who learn to visualize data effectively gain a new kind of literacy — one that combines analytical thinking with creative communication. They learn not only how to interpret numbers but also how to express what those numbers mean.

Visualization and Transparency in AI

One of the most important uses of visualization in artificial intelligence is promoting **transparency**. AI systems often operate in ways that are difficult to understand — a problem known as the "black box" issue. Visualization opens that box by showing how inputs lead to outputs. For example, visualizing which parts of an image a neural network focuses on during recognition can reveal whether the model is learning correctly or being misled by irrelevant details. This transparency builds trust between humans and machines.

Teachers can use this concept to discuss how visual evidence builds understanding in all subjects — from history timelines to science charts. In the age of AI, being able to read and interpret visual information has become as essential as reading text.

Data Visualization in Everyday Life

Students already encounter data visualization in many forms: weather maps, health trackers, financial dashboards, and even social media statistics. These everyday visuals help them make sense of the world — deciding what to wear, how to save money, or how to improve their fitness goals. In the classroom, teachers can encourage students to create their own charts from real data, such as school surveys, local environmental readings, or class projects. This hands-on experience turns abstract numbers into meaningful discoveries.

Visualization also helps explain global topics like population growth, climate patterns, or economic trends. When complex information becomes visible, it becomes accessible — empowering people of all ages to make informed decisions.

Seeing the Bigger Picture

Data visualization reminds us that learning is not just about memorizing facts — it's about *seeing connections*. In AI, visualization transforms enormous datasets into stories that can guide action, solve problems, and spark innovation. It encourages students to look closer, think critically, and see beauty in information. When numbers become pictures, understanding becomes universal.

In the next chapter, we'll explore how those visual and data-driven insights come alive in the real world — through **applications of AI and neural networks in everyday life**, from healthcare and education to art, communication, and environmental science.

Chapter 13 Reflection

This chapter helps students understand that numbers alone do not always tell a clear story. Data visualization allows humans to *see* patterns, changes, and relationships that might otherwise remain hidden. Reflecting on this idea helps students realize that understanding information often depends on how it is presented, not just what it contains.

Students are encouraged to think about how visuals influence their understanding every day. Weather maps, charts in class, and graphs on apps all help turn complex data into something understandable. This reflection shows that visualization is a powerful learning tool, not just a design choice.

The chapter also invites students to see visualization as a bridge between humans and machines. By turning AI data into visuals, people can better understand, question, and trust intelligent systems.

Chapter 13 Summary

Data visualization is the process of turning numbers into visual forms such as charts, graphs, and maps so humans can understand information more easily. Because the human brain processes images faster than text or raw data, visualization helps reveal patterns, trends, and relationships that might otherwise go unnoticed. In artificial intelligence, visualization is essential for understanding how models learn and perform.

Different visualization tools serve different purposes. Bar charts compare categories, line graphs show changes over time, pie charts display proportions, scatter plots reveal relationships, and heat maps show intensity using color. In AI systems, specialized visuals such as loss curves and confusion matrices help engineers see how well a model is learning and where it needs improvement.

Visualization is also a tool for transparency and trust. By showing how AI systems make decisions, visualization helps reduce the "black box" problem and allows humans to evaluate whether a system is learning correctly or unfairly. Beyond AI, data visualization plays a major role in everyday life—from health tracking to climate data—helping people make informed decisions. Understanding visualization gives students a powerful skill for interpreting information and communicating insights clearly.

Chapter 13 Quiz

1. What is data visualization?
2. Why are visuals easier for humans to understand than raw numbers?
3. What type of chart is best for showing change over time?
4. What does a bar chart help compare?
5. What is the purpose of a scatter plot?
6. How does data visualization help AI engineers?
7. What is meant by the "black box" problem in AI?
8. How can visualization improve trust in AI systems?
9. Name one way students encounter data visualization in daily life.
10. Why is data visualization considered both science and creativity?

Chapter 13 Worksheet

Part A: Understanding Visual Tools

1. Match the visualization type to its best use:
   - Bar Chart
   - Line Graph
   - Pie Chart
   - Heat Map
2. Give one real-world example where data visualization is useful.

Part B: Thinking Critically

3. Why might looking at raw numbers be confusing without visuals?
4. How can poor visualization lead to misunderstanding?

Part C: Reflection

5. Describe a time when a chart or graph helped you understand something better.
6. Why is it important for students to learn how to read and create data visuals?

Chapter 13 Answer Key

Quiz Answers

1. Turning data into visual forms to show patterns and meaning
2. The brain processes images faster than numbers
3. A line graph
4. Different categories or groups
5. To show relationships between variables
6. It helps them monitor learning and find problems
7. When AI decisions are hard to understand
8. It shows how decisions are made
9. Weather maps, fitness trackers, social media stats, charts in class
10. It combines logical analysis with visual communication

Worksheet Sample Answers

(Answers may vary)

1.

- Bar Chart → Compare categories
- Line Graph → Show trends over time
- Pie Chart → Show proportions
- Heat Map → Show intensity with color

2. Tracking grades, weather forecasts, or sports statistics.
3. Numbers alone don't clearly show patterns.
4. It can hide trends or exaggerate results.
5. Graphs can make changes or comparisons easier to see.
6. It builds critical thinking and communication skills.

Chapter 14: Applications of Artificial Neural Networks in Everyday Life

Artificial Neural Networks (ANNs) have moved from research laboratories into the heart of everyday life. Once a complex idea studied by computer scientists, neural networks now power many of the tools, services, and devices that people use daily — often without even realizing it. From unlocking smartphones with your face to getting real-time directions or watching personalized video recommendations, **neural networks are quietly transforming how we live, learn, and communicate.**

These systems are modeled after the human brain — capable of recognizing patterns, learning from examples, and improving over time. Their ability to process large amounts of data and discover hidden relationships makes them invaluable across every industry. What once seemed futuristic has become part of ordinary experience, bridging the gap between human intelligence and machine capability.

1. Neural Networks in Communication

Every time we use voice assistants like Siri, Alexa, or Google Assistant, a neural network is at work. These systems use **speech recognition models** to convert spoken words into text and **natural language processing** to understand meaning. The same technology translates languages in real time, enabling people across the world to communicate seamlessly.

In texting apps and emails, neural networks predict the next word you intend to type and even suggest replies — saving time and improving efficiency. Behind every smart reply or autocorrect feature lies a machine that has learned language patterns by analyzing millions of sentences. This technology is transforming how people communicate and connect across cultures and languages.

2. Neural Networks in Education

In classrooms, neural networks are helping teachers and students personalize learning. **AI-driven tutoring systems** analyze a student's strengths and weaknesses to suggest customized lessons or practice exercises. These intelligent systems adapt to the learner's pace — offering extra help where needed and advanced material when mastery is shown.

Neural networks also assist in grading essays, detecting plagiarism, and tracking student progress. This allows teachers to focus more on mentoring and creativity instead of routine administrative tasks. The classroom of the future will not replace teachers with machines rather, it will pair teachers with intelligent assistants that help each student reach their full potential.

3. Neural Networks in Healthcare

Healthcare has been revolutionized by neural networks that assist doctors in diagnosis and treatment. **Convolutional Neural Networks (CNNs)** are used to analyze X-rays, MRIs, and CT scans to detect tumors, fractures, or infections with incredible precision. In some cases, AI systems can identify patterns invisible to the human eye, helping save lives through early detection.

Other networks predict patient outcomes, assist in drug discovery, and even help design personalized treatment plans. For example, recurrent neural networks (RNNs) analyze patient history to anticipate potential health risks. This combination of human expertise and machine intelligence is building a new era of smarter, faster, and more accurate medicine.

4. Neural Networks in Transportation

When you open a navigation app like Google Maps or Waze, neural networks are working behind the scenes to predict traffic flow, suggest alternate routes, and estimate travel times. In **self-driving cars**, neural networks play an even bigger role — helping vehicles see through cameras, detect pedestrians, read road signs, and make split-second decisions.

These systems combine visual processing (through CNNs) with decision-making algorithms (through reinforcement learning) to navigate safely. The ultimate goal is to reduce human error, improve road safety, and make transportation more efficient for everyone.

5. Neural Networks in Entertainment

In music, movies, and social media, neural networks curate personalized experiences. Streaming services like Netflix, Spotify, and YouTube analyze your viewing or listening habits to recommend new content you're likely to enjoy. These systems rely on **recommendation algorithms** powered by deep learning, which identify subtle similarities between users and preferences.

Neural networks also enable **AI art and creativity** — composing original music, painting digital artworks, and even generating realistic human voices. These creative applications show that intelligence isn't limited to numbers and data; it can also express imagination and emotion.

6. Neural Networks in Finance and Business

Financial institutions use neural networks to detect fraud, manage investments, and automate trading. For example, AI systems can recognize unusual spending patterns that might indicate stolen credit cards. In business, neural networks analyze customer behavior, forecast demand, and optimize pricing strategies.

Chatbots powered by neural networks provide 24/7 customer support, helping answer questions or resolve issues instantly. These systems are not just about saving time — they also improve accuracy and consistency in service, building trust between companies and customers.

7. Neural Networks in Environmental Science

Neural networks also play a vital role in protecting our planet. Scientists use them to predict natural disasters like floods, earthquakes, and hurricanes. Satellite imagery analyzed by deep learning models helps track deforestation, monitor ocean temperatures, and measure air pollution.

By processing massive datasets from sensors and satellites, AI provides early warnings that save lives and guide policy decisions. This blend of intelligence and environmental stewardship shows how technology can work in harmony with nature.

8. Neural Networks in Everyday Devices

Modern smartphones, cameras, and home appliances all rely on AI. Cameras use neural networks to enhance photos, remove noise, and automatically detect faces. Smart refrigerators monitor food freshness, while thermostats learn your habits to conserve energy. Even vacuum robots use neural networks to map rooms and avoid obstacles. These everyday conveniences are silent examples of machine learning improving comfort, safety, and efficiency in our daily lives.

Bringing It All Together

Artificial Neural Networks have become **the invisible companions of modern living**. They assist, predict, guide, and create — often without us noticing. Yet behind every intelligent system lies human curiosity and design. These networks reflect our collective effort to understand intelligence itself and to use it for the betterment of humanity.

For teachers, this chapter offers opportunities for engaging classroom projects: students can research how AI is used in a field they care about — sports, music, healthcare, or gaming — and present its impact. Such activities build awareness that AI is not just a topic for engineers; it's a living part of the world every student inhabits.

Neural networks are no longer the future — they are the **present**, shaping the way we think, work, and dream.

In the next chapter, we will explore one of the most essential aspects of this transformation — **Ethical and Responsible AI**, where intelligence meets morality, and technology learns the meaning of responsibility.

Chapter 14 Reflection

This chapter helps students recognize that artificial neural networks are already part of their everyday lives. Many tools students use daily — phones, apps, navigation systems, and streaming platforms — rely on neural networks to function intelligently. Reflecting on this idea helps students see AI as something familiar rather than distant or mysterious.

Students are encouraged to think about how neural networks assist humans rather than replace them. In education, healthcare, transportation, and communication, AI works alongside people to improve accuracy, efficiency, and safety. This reflection highlights the idea that technology is most powerful when it supports human goals.

The chapter also invites students to consider responsibility. Because neural networks influence so many areas of life, understanding how they work helps students become informed users and thoughtful citizens in an AI-driven world.

Chapter 14 Summary

Artificial Neural Networks have moved beyond research labs and into everyday life. These systems, inspired by the human brain, can recognize patterns, learn from experience, and improve over time. Their ability to process large amounts of data makes them useful across many industries, from communication and education to healthcare and environmental science.

In communication, neural networks power voice assistants, language translation, predictive text, and smart replies. In education, they personalize learning, assist with grading, and help teachers track student progress. Healthcare systems use neural networks to analyze medical images, predict outcomes, and support early diagnosis. In transportation, they guide navigation systems and enable self-driving technologies that aim to improve safety and efficiency.

Neural networks also shape entertainment, finance, business, and environmental protection. They recommend music and videos, detect fraud, optimize business decisions, and help scientists monitor climate change and natural disasters. Even everyday devices such as smartphones, cameras, thermostats, and home robots rely on neural networks to function intelligently. Together, these applications show that neural networks are not futuristic ideas — they are practical tools shaping modern life.

Chapter 14 Quiz

1. What are Artificial Neural Networks (ANNs)?
2. Why are neural networks compared to the human brain?
3. How do neural networks help people communicate?
4. Name one way neural networks are used in education.
5. How do neural networks support healthcare professionals?
6. What role do neural networks play in transportation?
7. How are neural networks used in entertainment platforms?
8. Why are neural networks important in finance and business?
9. How do neural networks help protect the environment?
10. Why is it important for students to understand AI applications in daily life?

Chapter 14 Worksheet

Part A: Understanding Everyday AI

1. List three areas of everyday life where neural networks are used.
2. Choose one area and briefly describe how AI helps in that field.

Part B: Thinking Critically

3. Why is AI described as an assistant rather than a replacement for humans?
4. What could happen if people rely on AI without understanding how it works?

Part C: Reflection

5. Which AI application do you use most often, and how does it help you?
6. Why should students learn about AI even if they don't plan to become engineers?

Chapter 14 Answer Key

Quiz Answers

1. AI systems that learn patterns from data
2. Because they process information in a similar learning-based way
3. Through voice recognition, translation, and text prediction
4. Personalized learning or automated grading
5. By analyzing images, predicting outcomes, and assisting diagnosis
6. Navigation, traffic prediction, and self-driving decisions
7. By recommending music, videos, and content
8. Detecting fraud and analyzing customer behavior
9. Predicting disasters and monitoring environmental data
10. AI affects daily decisions and society

Worksheet Sample Answers

(Answers may vary)

1. Communication, healthcare, entertainment.
2. In education, AI adapts lessons to student needs.
3. AI supports human decision-making.
4. Mistakes, bias, or misuse could occur.
5. Navigation apps or streaming recommendations.
6. AI impacts all careers and daily life.

Chapter 15: Ethical and Responsible AI

Artificial Intelligence has become one of the most powerful forces shaping our world. It helps doctors save lives, teachers personalize learning, and companies solve complex problems. Yet with great power comes great responsibility. As machines learn to make decisions, humans must ensure that those decisions align with fairness, truth, and compassion. This is the heart of **Ethical and Responsible AI** — a movement to build systems that not only think intelligently but also act wisely.

Ethical AI means teaching machines to respect human values. It involves asking deep questions about what is right, fair, and just in the digital age. How should AI treat private data? How do we prevent discrimination in algorithms? How do we make sure machines serve humanity instead of replacing it? These questions are not just for engineers — they are for everyone, from students and teachers to business leaders and citizens. Ethics in AI is a shared duty to guide technology toward the good of all.

The Foundations of Ethical AI

At its core, ethical AI is built on a few fundamental principles that guide responsible development:

1. **Fairness:** AI must treat all individuals and groups equally, without bias or prejudice. This means ensuring that training data reflects diversity and that algorithms do not unfairly favor or exclude anyone.
2. **Transparency:** People should be able to understand how AI systems make their decisions. This involves clear explanations, open data practices, and honest communication about limitations.
3. **Accountability:** Developers and organizations must take responsibility for the outcomes of their AI systems. When mistakes occur, there must be ways to correct them and prevent future harm.
4. **Privacy and Security:** AI must respect personal information and protect it from misuse. Data should be collected ethically, stored safely, and used only for its intended purpose.
5. **Human Oversight:** Machines should support human judgment, not replace it. Critical decisions — especially in healthcare, education, or justice — must always involve human review.

These principles form the ethical compass of modern AI, ensuring that progress never comes at the cost of human dignity or trust.

When AI Goes Wrong

AI is not perfect, and when it fails, the consequences can be serious. Bias in hiring algorithms can exclude qualified candidates. Facial recognition systems can misidentify people, leading to unfair treatment. Predictive policing tools might reinforce existing inequalities if trained on biased historical data. These issues remind us that technology reflects the values of its creators — if we are not careful, our machines can mirror our mistakes.

Teachers can use these real-world examples to inspire discussion about responsibility. Just as students must learn from errors in judgment, so must engineers and scientists learn from the ethical challenges of AI. The goal is not to fear technology, but to **teach it to care** — to embed fairness and empathy within its code.

AI and Human Values

For AI to serve humanity, it must be designed around **human-centered values**. This means asking questions that go beyond efficiency: Does this system help people live better lives? Does it strengthen community trust? Does it protect freedom and creativity? These questions remind us that intelligence without ethics is incomplete.

Ethical AI recognizes that humans are more than data points. Our emotions, beliefs, and cultures shape how we define right and wrong. When machines make decisions, they must do so with respect for these differences. This human-centered approach ensures that AI serves as a partner in progress — not a ruler over it.

The Role of Education in Ethical AI

Schools play a vital role in shaping the next generation of ethical innovators. By teaching students about AI responsibility, educators prepare them to think critically about the impact of technology on society. Lessons in **digital citizenship**, **data ethics**, and **algorithmic fairness** help students understand that AI is not just about coding — it's about conscience.

Teachers can encourage classroom debates, role-playing activities, or creative projects where students design their own "ethical AI guidelines." Such experiences help young minds connect morality with innovation. They learn that being a good technologist also means being a good human.

Building Trust Between Humans and Machines

Trust is the foundation of every relationship — including the one between people and technology. When AI operates transparently, safely, and fairly, people are more likely to embrace it. But when it behaves unpredictably or violates privacy, trust is broken. Responsible AI seeks to build long-term confidence by proving that intelligence can coexist with integrity.

Organizations that practice ethical AI are open about their methods, welcome feedback, and remain accountable for outcomes. This culture of honesty and reflection ensures that machines enhance — rather than undermine — the human experience.

A Shared Future

Ethical and Responsible AI is not a destination; it is a continuous journey. As technology evolves, new challenges will emerge — and humanity must respond with wisdom, compassion, and courage. The machines we build will always mirror the values we teach them. If we choose fairness, truth, and empathy, AI will carry those same values into the future.

For students, this chapter serves as a reminder that **ethics is not a barrier to innovation — it is its backbone**. For teachers, it offers a path to connect moral reasoning with scientific discovery. Together, they form the foundation of a new generation of ethical thinkers ready to lead the intelligent age.

In the next chapter, we will explore **The Future of Neural Networks — Quantum and Beyond**, where we imagine how the next frontier of computation may push artificial intelligence toward entirely new dimensions of learning and thought.

Chapter 15 Reflection

This chapter reminds students that intelligence alone is not enough. As artificial intelligence becomes more powerful, humans must guide it with values such as fairness, honesty, and responsibility. Reflecting on ethical AI helps students understand that machines do not decide what is right or wrong on their own — people do.

Students are encouraged to think about how technology affects real lives. When AI makes decisions in areas like education, healthcare, or justice, mistakes can cause real harm. This reflection shows that ethical thinking must always be part of innovation.

The chapter also invites students to see themselves as future decision-makers. Whether they become engineers, teachers, business leaders, or citizens, their choices will shape how AI is used. Ethical responsibility belongs to everyone, not just programmers.

Chapter 15 Summary

Ethical and Responsible AI focuses on ensuring that artificial intelligence systems act in ways that align with human values. While AI has the power to improve lives through better healthcare, education, and communication, it also carries risks if used without care. Ethical AI asks important questions about fairness, transparency, privacy, accountability, and human oversight.

The foundations of ethical AI include treating all people fairly, explaining how decisions are made, protecting personal data, and ensuring humans remain involved in critical decisions. When these principles are ignored, AI systems can cause harm, such as biased hiring tools, inaccurate facial recognition, or unfair predictive systems. These failures show that AI reflects the values of its creators and the data it learns from.

Education plays a key role in building ethical AI. By teaching students about responsibility, fairness, and digital citizenship, schools prepare the next generation to guide technology wisely. Ethical AI is not about slowing progress — it is about ensuring that innovation serves humanity with trust, integrity, and compassion.

Chapter 15 Quiz

1. What is Ethical and Responsible AI?
2. Why does AI require human guidance?

3. What does fairness mean in AI systems?
4. Why is transparency important in AI?
5. What is accountability in AI development?
6. Why must AI respect privacy and security?
7. What does human oversight mean?
8. Give one example of when AI can cause harm.
9. Why is education important for ethical AI?
10. How can ethical AI help build trust with society?

Chapter 15 Worksheet

Part A: Understanding Ethical Principles

1. List three principles of ethical AI and explain them briefly.
2. Why is fairness a key concern in AI systems?

Part B: Thinking Critically

3. What could happen if AI systems make decisions without human oversight?
4. How can transparency help people trust AI?

Part C: Reflection

5. How should AI be used to support humans rather than replace them?
6. Why do you think ethics is important in future technology careers?

Chapter 15 Answer Key

Quiz Answers

1. AI that follows human values and responsibility
2. Machines do not understand morality on their own
3. Treating all people equally and without bias
4. So people can understand how decisions are made
5. Taking responsibility for AI outcomes
6. To protect personal information
7. Humans reviewing and guiding AI decisions
8. Biased hiring or incorrect facial recognition
9. It teaches responsibility and critical thinking
10. It ensures AI acts fairly and predictably

Worksheet Sample Answers

(Answers may vary)

1. Fairness (equal treatment), transparency (clear decisions), privacy (data protection).
2. Unfair data can lead to discrimination.
3. Harmful or incorrect decisions could occur.
4. People can see and understand the reasoning.
5. AI should assist, not replace, human judgment.
6. Technology affects real people and society.

Chapter 16: The Future of Neural Networks — Quantum and Beyond

The story of Artificial Neural Networks is far from over. In fact, it is only beginning. Just as the human brain continues to surprise us with its complexity and creativity, the future of machine intelligence holds limitless possibilities. Scientists and engineers are now exploring new frontiers that combine classical computing with the strange and powerful world of **quantum mechanics**. This next stage of evolution is leading to the rise of **Quantum Neural Networks (QNNs)** and other advanced architectures that could redefine the meaning of intelligence itself.

The Next Frontier: Quantum Intelligence

In classical computing, information is processed in **bits** — zeros and ones — the simple foundation of digital logic. In quantum computing, however, information is processed in **qubits**, which can exist as both zero and one at the same time, thanks to a phenomenon called **superposition**. This ability allows quantum computers to perform many calculations simultaneously, making them potentially far faster and more powerful than any machine that exists today.

When combined with neural networks, this creates the concept of **Quantum Neural Networks** — systems capable of learning, adapting, and reasoning in ways that classical computers cannot. Instead of processing data in fixed sequences, quantum networks explore multiple possibilities at once. They can analyze massive datasets, detect hidden correlations, and optimize solutions in fields like chemistry, medicine, and physics with unprecedented efficiency.

Students can think of this transformation as moving from a one-lane road to a multi-dimensional highway — where data travels in every possible direction at once, discovering patterns that traditional AI might never see.

Biological Inspiration and Beyond

The next generation of neural networks will not only rely on quantum mechanics but also on **biology, neuroscience, and evolution**. Scientists are studying how real neurons in the brain form, adapt, and repair themselves, hoping to design **self-healing, self-organizing AI systems**.

These networks could rewire themselves when damaged, learn continuously without retraining, and even transfer knowledge between machines — similar to how humans share ideas.

This vision moves AI from being a static tool to a **living system** — one that grows, remembers, and evolves. Researchers call this the era of *neuromorphic computing*, where hardware mimics the structure and function of biological brains. Imagine a processor that doesn't just calculate but **feels patterns**, storing sensory experiences like touch, sound, or sight in real-time. These systems would make machines more adaptable, energy-efficient, and emotionally aware of their surroundings.

AI and the Expanding Universe of Learning

The future of neural networks extends beyond Earth itself. In space exploration, AI systems already guide rovers on Mars and analyze data from distant stars. Future generations of AI could help astronauts predict cosmic radiation, navigate deep-space missions, or even communicate with autonomous robotic colonies on other planets. Neural networks will act as **co-pilots of discovery**, carrying human knowledge to places where humans cannot yet go.

On Earth, AI will continue to merge with robotics, energy systems, and climate science. Neural networks will predict environmental changes, optimize renewable energy, and monitor the planet's health. In medicine, they will design treatments tailored to each person's unique genetic makeup. In education, they will become personal mentors for every student — learning how each brain learns best.

Quantum Neural Networks and Conscious Computing

The question many scientists now ask is: *Can machines one day become conscious?* While true consciousness remains uniquely human, the growing sophistication of neural networks suggests that future machines could achieve **awareness-like behavior** — systems that understand goals, consequences, and even emotions in a limited sense.

Quantum Neural Networks may bring us closer to this threshold. Because they operate in a probabilistic rather than deterministic way, they can model uncertainty, intuition, and creativity — qualities once thought to be purely human. This doesn't mean machines will "feel" as we do, but they could understand emotional data well enough to respond with empathy, such as comforting a patient or supporting a student's learning challenges.

The merging of quantum logic and emotional intelligence could mark the dawn of **Conscious Computing**, where machines are not just intelligent, but also context-aware, reflective, and ethical.

Challenges on the Horizon

Despite these exciting advancements, the road ahead is filled with challenges. Quantum computers are still in their early stages — expensive, fragile, and limited in scale. Building stable qubits that can store and process information without interference is one of science's greatest challenges. Similarly, ethical and environmental concerns will grow as AI becomes more powerful. How do we ensure that advanced intelligence remains beneficial and sustainable? How do we maintain human oversight when machines begin to make complex decisions independently?

These questions remind us that progress must be guided by **ethics, wisdom, and humility**. Technology can be a force for good only when paired with moral awareness and global cooperation.

Education and the Future Generation

The students of today will be the architects of this quantum future. By learning how machines think, they prepare themselves not just to use technology, but to **shape it**. Teachers play an essential role in this transformation — helping students see AI not as a mystery, but as a field of creativity, responsibility, and endless discovery.

Classroom discussions about the future of neural networks should spark imagination: What if students designed the next generation of ethical AI? What if they helped solve climate change using quantum intelligence? What if they built systems that learn as beautifully as the human mind does? These are not science-fiction questions — they are invitations to invent the next era of knowledge.

The Journey Continues

As we move from neural networks to quantum networks, from artificial intelligence to intelligent collaboration, humanity stands at the edge of a new age — one where learning never ends. The machines of the future will not replace us; they will **reflect us** — our logic, our creativity, our compassion, and our endless curiosity.

Neural networks began as mathematical experiments. Today, they are the beating heart of intelligent machines. Tomorrow, they may become the architects of discoveries we cannot yet imagine. The future of AI will be written not only in code but in **conscious understanding** — the shared dialogue between human and machine, thought and quantum possibility, science and imagination.

Closing Reflection for Students and Teachers

The future belongs to thinkers who balance intelligence with integrity. For students, this means dreaming boldly and learning deeply. For teachers, it means guiding with empathy and vision. Together, they can ensure that the next generation of intelligence — whether human or artificial — grows with purpose, fairness, and wonder.

As we step into the quantum horizon, one truth remains: **The power of intelligence, in all its forms, is most beautiful when used to uplift humanity.**

Chapter 16 Reflection

This chapter invites students to imagine the future of intelligence beyond what exists today. It shows that artificial intelligence is not finished evolving — it is entering a new phase that blends technology, biology, and even quantum science. Reflecting on this chapter helps students understand that the future of AI will be shaped by human choices, curiosity, and responsibility.

Students are encouraged to think about intelligence as something that grows and adapts. Just as humans learn throughout their lives, future neural networks may learn continuously, repair themselves, and respond more thoughtfully to the world. This reflection highlights that progress in AI is not just about speed or power, but about wisdom and care.

The chapter also asks students to see themselves as future builders of this world. The next generation will decide how advanced intelligence is used — for healing, learning, protecting the planet, and exploring the universe. Reflection helps students recognize that the future of AI is not something that happens *to* them, but something they help create.

Chapter 16 Summary

The future of neural networks extends far beyond today's technology. Scientists are exploring new forms of intelligence that combine classical computing with quantum mechanics, biology, and neuroscience. Quantum Neural Networks use qubits instead of traditional bits, allowing machines to process many possibilities at once. This could lead to breakthroughs in medicine, chemistry, climate science, and space exploration by solving problems too complex for classical computers.

Beyond quantum computing, researchers are designing systems inspired by the human brain. These future networks may be self-healing, adaptive, and capable of learning continuously without restarting training. Neuromorphic computing aims to build hardware that behaves like biological neurons, making AI more efficient and flexible. These systems could respond to real-world environments with greater awareness and sensitivity.

As neural networks grow more powerful, ethical responsibility becomes even more important. Challenges such as fairness, sustainability, and human oversight must guide development. Education plays a critical role in preparing students to understand and shape this future. By combining imagination with ethics, humanity can ensure that future intelligence — whether artificial or quantum — serves the common good and reflects our highest values.

Chapter 16 Quiz

1. Why is the story of neural networks considered unfinished?
2. What is a qubit, and how is it different from a bit?
3. What is a Quantum Neural Network (QNN)?
4. How could quantum computing change AI learning?
5. What is neuromorphic computing?
6. Why are scientists studying the human brain to design AI?

7. How might future AI help in space exploration?
8. What is meant by "conscious-like" or awareness-based computing?
9. What challenges must be addressed as AI becomes more powerful?
10. Why do students play an important role in the future of AI?

Chapter 16 Worksheet

Part A: Understanding the Future

1. Describe one way quantum computing could improve artificial intelligence.
2. Explain how future neural networks may be different from today's systems.

Part B: Thinking Critically

3. Why is ethics important when developing advanced AI technologies?
4. How could AI help solve global problems like climate change or healthcare?

Part C: Reflection

5. How do you imagine AI helping humans in the future?
6. What responsibility do future innovators have when creating intelligent systems?

Chapter 16 Answer Key

Quiz Answers

1. AI is still evolving and expanding into new areas
2. A qubit can be both 0 and 1 at the same time
3. A neural network that uses quantum computing principles
4. It allows faster and more complex learning
5. Computing inspired by biological brains
6. To make AI more adaptive and efficient
7. Navigation, data analysis, and mission planning
8. AI that understands context and emotional data
9. Ethics, safety, and sustainability
10. They will design and guide future technology

Worksheet Sample Answers

(Answers may vary)

1. Quantum AI can analyze many possibilities at once.
2. They may learn continuously and repair themselves.
3. Powerful AI can cause harm if not guided responsibly.
4. Predicting climate changes or creating personalized medicine.
5. Assisting learning, healthcare, or exploration.
6. To ensure AI benefits humanity fairly.

Closing Note

This chapter serves as a **visionary conclusion** to your AI literacy journey. It reminds students and teachers that intelligence — human or artificial — is most powerful when guided by curiosity, ethics, and compassion.

🎓 Benefits for Students

Learning about **Data: Fuel for Artificial Neurons** opens a world of curiosity and understanding. This textbook helps students see how intelligence is built, not just in machines, but in all systems that learn and adapt. Through every chapter, learners discover how information becomes knowledge and how patterns in data mirror the way their own brains work.

Students who complete this book will:

- Develop a foundational understanding of **how data powers AI**, and how it transforms raw numbers into intelligent behavior.
- Strengthen their **critical thinking and problem-solving skills** by exploring how machines process, analyze, and learn from data.
- Gain awareness of **ethical and responsible data practices**, understanding the importance of fairness, accuracy, and privacy in the digital world.
- Learn how **mathematics, science, and technology connect**, bridging what they study in the classroom to real-world innovation.
- Be inspired to pursue future studies or careers in **artificial intelligence, data science, engineering, and computer technology**.

Most importantly, this book teaches that intelligence — whether human or artificial — begins with curiosity. Every dataset, every equation, and every neural network starts with a question: *What can we learn from this?* Students will walk away understanding that they, too, are part of this great journey of discovery.

Benefits for Teachers

For educators, this textbook serves as a bridge between traditional learning and the digital age. It is not just a guide to technology but a **curriculum for understanding modern intelligence** — accessible, classroom-friendly, and aligned with 21st-century learning goals.

Teachers using this book will find it valuable for:

- Introducing **STEM and AI literacy** in a way that is engaging, visual, and discussion-based.
- Encouraging students to think critically about **how machines learn and make decisions**, linking concepts from math, science, and ethics.
- Providing ready-to-use classroom examples, analogies, and discussion points that connect lessons to students' daily experiences.
- Supporting **interdisciplinary education**, combining computer science with language, art, and social studies to show AI's broader human impact.
- Inspiring project-based learning — from data collection experiments to visualizing datasets, coding simple neural models, or exploring AI ethics through debate and writing.

This book allows teachers to be both guides and explorers — leading students through the evolving world of AI while learning alongside them. It encourages collaboration, creativity, and curiosity — values at the heart of lifelong learning.

1. Understanding the Basics

1. Why is data considered the "fuel" for artificial neurons?
2. Explain how data is transformed into learning within an AI system.
3. What role do weights and biases play in a neural network?

2. Inside the Machine Brain

4. How does backpropagation help a machine improve its accuracy over time?
5. What is the difference between a neuron "firing" in a biological brain and in an artificial one?
6. Why are activation functions important for creating non-linear intelligence?

3. Real-World Connections

7. Describe one real-world example of how neural networks are used in everyday life.
8. How do GPUs and TPUs help AI systems learn faster?
9. Why is training data quality so important for fairness and accuracy in AI?

4. Ethics and Responsibility

10. Define "bias" in artificial intelligence and describe one way it can appear in data.
11. Why is transparency important in building trust between humans and AI systems?
12. How can students and teachers promote responsible AI development in their own schools?

5. Looking Ahead

13. What are Quantum Neural Networks, and how might they change the future of learning?
14. Describe how neuromorphic computing draws inspiration from the human brain.
15. In your opinion, what is the most important quality that future AI systems should have — and why?

Bonus Reflection

Essay Prompt:
"Data gives machines the power to think, but humanity gives them the purpose to care."
— Reflect on what this means to you as a student living in the age of intelligent technology.

Teacher Tip:
Encourage students to discuss their answers in small groups before writing. This promotes collaboration, deep reflection, and the realization that **learning about AI is not just about machines — it's about understanding what it means to be human in a digital world.**

GLOSSARY

Letter A

1. Access Time

The amount of time it takes for an AI system or computer to locate and retrieve data from memory or storage. Access time affects how quickly megabytes of data can be used during AI processing.

2. Activation Data

Intermediate data generated inside an AI model while it is running. Activation data is stored temporarily in memory and often measured in megabytes during model execution.

3. Adaptive Storage

A storage approach that automatically adjusts how data is stored or moved based on usage patterns. In AI systems, adaptive storage helps manage large volumes of megabytes efficiently.

4.Agentic AI:
A form of AI behavior where intelligent systems can plan, adapt, make decisions, and perform multi-step actions with limited human guidance.

5.AI Agent:
An AI-powered system designed to observe information, make decisions, and take actions to complete specific tasks or goals.

6.AI (Artificial Intelligence):
A branch of computer science that allows machines and software systems to perform tasks that normally require human intelligence, such as learning, reasoning, problem-solving, and decision-making.

7.AI Autonomy (Autonomy AI):
The level of independence an AI system has when operating, making decisions, or completing tasks without constant human control.

8.AI Autonomous Worker:
An advanced AI system capable of independently performing work-related tasks, managing workflows, and completing objectives with minimal human supervision.

9. Algorithmic Data Size

The total amount of data an algorithm needs to operate effectively. In AI, this size is often measured in megabytes or larger units, depending on model complexity.

10. Allocation (Memory Allocation)

The process of assigning a specific number of megabytes in memory or storage for an AI task, model, or dataset.

11. Analytics Dataset

A structured collection of data used for analysis or AI training. The size of an analytics dataset is commonly measured in megabytes, gigabytes, or more.

12. Annotation Storage

The space required to store labels, tags, or explanations added to AI training data. These annotations contribute additional megabytes to total dataset size.

13. Artificial Neural Network (ANN) Size

The total memory footprint of a neural network, including weights, biases, and parameters. ANN size is often described in megabytes when discussing model efficiency.

14. Asset Compression

The process of reducing the number of megabytes required to store AI-related files such as models, images, or datasets without losing essential information.

15. Available Memory

The amount of free memory, measured in megabytes, that an AI system can still use to load data, run models, or perform computations.

16.ANI (Artificial Narrow Intelligence)

Artificial Narrow Intelligence refers to AI systems designed to perform **one specific task or a narrow set of tasks** rather than general intelligence. ANI systems rely on data stored and processed in memory and storage measured in **megabytes, gigabytes, or more**. Examples include image recognition, speech-to-text, recommendation systems, and chatbots. ANI does not understand beyond its training scope, but it can process large amounts of data efficiently within its defined function.

Letter B

1. Bandwidth

The amount of data that can be transferred between systems in a given time. In AI systems, bandwidth determines how quickly megabytes of data can move between storage, memory, and processors.

2. Batch Processing

A method where AI systems process large groups of data all at once instead of one item at a time. Batch processing often involves handling many megabytes of data in a single operation.

3. Binary Encoding

The process of representing information using binary values (0s and 1s). All megabytes of AI data are ultimately stored and transmitted using binary encoding.

4. Bit Depth

The number of bits used to represent a single piece of data, such as a pixel or audio sample. Higher bit depth increases data quality but also increases the number of megabytes required.

5. Bitmap Data

A type of image data where each pixel is stored as a set of bits. Bitmap images can quickly grow in size, consuming large numbers of megabytes in AI vision systems.

6. Buffer Memory

Temporary memory used to hold data while it is being transferred or processed. Buffers store data in chunks measured in megabytes to keep AI systems running smoothly.

7. Bulk Data Storage

Large-scale storage designed to hold massive datasets used for AI training or analysis. Bulk storage capacity is measured in megabytes, gigabytes, or larger units.

8. Byte Stream

A continuous flow of bytes transmitted or processed by a system. AI applications often analyze byte streams that accumulate into megabytes of data.

9. Bytecode

An intermediate form of program code that is easier for machines to execute than human-written code. Bytecode files occupy storage space measured in megabytes.

10. Byzantine Fault Tolerance (BFT)

A system property that allows AI or distributed systems to continue functioning even when some components fail or act unpredictably. Implementing BFT requires additional data handling and storage overhead measured in megabytes.

Letter C

1. Cache Memory

A small, high-speed memory area that stores frequently used data so the processor can access it faster. Cache helps reduce the time needed to move megabytes of data from main memory or storage.

2. Capacity Planning

The process of estimating how much memory and storage an AI system will need. Capacity planning ensures there are enough megabytes available to handle data, models, and future growth.

3. Checkpoint File

A saved snapshot of an AI model during training. Checkpoint files are stored in memory or storage and often consume many megabytes so training can resume without starting over.

4. Chunking

The practice of breaking large datasets into smaller pieces. Chunking helps AI systems process megabytes of data more efficiently by handling them in manageable parts.

5. Cloud Storage

A method of storing data on remote servers accessed through the internet. Cloud storage manages files measured in megabytes and allows AI systems to scale beyond local hardware limits.

6. Compression

The process of reducing the size of data so it uses fewer megabytes. Compression helps AI systems store, transfer, and process data more efficiently.

7. Compute Load

The amount of processing work required to run an AI task. Compute load often increases as the number of megabytes being processed grows.

8. Context Window

The amount of data an AI model can consider at one time. Context windows consume memory measured in megabytes, especially in language and vision models.

9. Corpus

A large collection of text or data used to train AI models. A corpus is usually measured in megabytes or larger units depending on its size.

10. CUDA Memory

Specialized memory used by GPUs to accelerate AI computations. CUDA memory holds model data and intermediate results measured in megabytes during processing.

Letter D

1. Data Allocation

The process of assigning a specific amount of memory or storage for data use. In AI systems, data allocation determines how many megabytes are reserved for datasets, models, or tasks.

2. Data Buffer

A temporary storage area that holds data while it is being transferred or processed. Data buffers manage megabytes of information to keep AI systems running smoothly.

3. Data Compression

A technique used to reduce the size of data so it consumes fewer megabytes. AI systems use data compression to save storage space and speed up data transfer.

4. Data Footprint

The total amount of data an AI system uses, including datasets, models, and temporary files. A data footprint is measured in megabytes, gigabytes, or more.

5. Data Loader

A software component that loads data into memory for AI training or inference. Data loaders handle batches of data measured in megabytes.

6. Data Migration

The process of moving data from one storage system to another. During AI system upgrades, data migration may involve transferring large numbers of megabytes.

7. Data Throughput

The rate at which data is processed or transferred by a system. Higher throughput allows AI systems to move more megabytes efficiently.

8. Dataset Size

The total amount of data in a dataset used for AI training or testing. Dataset size is commonly measured in megabytes or larger units.

9. Deep Learning Model Size

The amount of memory required to store a deep learning model, including its parameters and weights. Model size is often described in megabytes to assess efficiency.

10. Disk Storage

Long-term storage used to save files, datasets, and AI models. Disk storage capacity and usage are measured in megabytes, gigabytes, or terabytes.

Letter E

1. Edge Computing

A computing approach where data is processed closer to where it is generated rather than sent to a central server. Edge computing reduces how many megabytes must be transferred over networks.

2. Embedding Size

The amount of memory required to store vector representations used by AI models. Embedding size is often measured in megabytes and affects model performance and storage needs.

3. Encoded Data

Data that has been converted into a specific format for storage or transmission. Encoded data occupies megabytes depending on the encoding method used.

4. Encoding Scheme

A rule set that defines how data is represented digitally, such as text or images. Different encoding schemes can increase or reduce the number of megabytes required.

5. Encrypted Storage

Storage that protects data by converting it into a secure format. Encryption may slightly increase the number of megabytes used due to added security information.

6. End-to-End Data Pipeline

The full path data takes from collection to processing and storage. Each stage of the pipeline manages data volumes measured in megabytes.

7. Energy Efficiency (AI Systems)

A measure of how much energy an AI system uses to process data. Systems that move and store fewer megabytes are often more energy efficient.

8. Execution Memory

The memory required while a program or AI model is running. Execution memory usage is tracked in megabytes during runtime.

9. External Storage

Storage devices located outside a computer, such as USB drives or external hard drives. External storage capacity is measured in megabytes and larger units.

10. Extracted Features

Important data patterns identified by AI models during processing. Extracted features are stored temporarily or permanently in memory measured in megabytes.

Letter F

1. Feature Map

A structured output produced by AI models, especially in image and signal processing. Feature maps are stored in memory and can consume significant megabytes during computation.

2. Feature Scaling

The process of adjusting data values to a consistent range before training an AI model. Feature scaling affects how efficiently megabytes of data are processed and stored.

3. File Allocation Table (FAT)

A file system structure that tracks where files are stored on a disk. FAT helps manage how megabytes are organized and retrieved from storage.

4. File Compression Format

A standardized way to reduce file size so it uses fewer megabytes. Compression formats help AI systems store and transfer data efficiently.

5. File System Cache

A temporary memory area that stores frequently accessed files. File system caches reduce repeated access to storage and manage megabytes more efficiently.

6. Floating-Point Data

Numerical data that includes decimal values and is commonly used in AI calculations. Floating-point data requires more bits per value, increasing memory usage measured in megabytes.

7. Frame Buffer

A region of memory that stores image or video frames before they are displayed or processed. Frame buffers often consume large numbers of megabytes in AI vision systems.

8. Fragmentation

A condition where data is stored in scattered locations instead of one continuous block. Fragmentation can reduce storage efficiency even when megabytes appear available.

9. Free Memory

The amount of unused memory available for programs or AI tasks. Free memory is measured in megabytes and determines how much additional data can be loaded.

10. Full Dataset Load

The act of loading an entire dataset into memory at once. This approach can require large amounts of megabytes and is common in AI training scenarios.

Letter G

1. Garbage Collection

An automatic memory-management process that frees memory no longer in use. Garbage collection helps reclaim megabytes so AI programs can continue running efficiently.

2. Generalization Data

Data used to test how well an AI model performs on new, unseen inputs. Storing and evaluating generalization data requires additional megabytes beyond training data.

3. Gigabyte (GB)

A larger unit of data measurement equal to 1,024 megabytes (or commonly approximated as 1,000 MB). Gigabytes are used when datasets or models grow beyond megabyte scale.

4. Graph Data Structure

A way of organizing data using nodes and connections. Graph-based AI systems store graph data in memory and storage measured in megabytes.

5. GPU Memory

Specialized memory used by graphics processing units to accelerate AI workloads. GPU memory holds model parameters and data batches measured in megabytes.

6. Gradient Data

Numerical values calculated during AI training to update model parameters. Gradient data is stored temporarily in memory and contributes to overall megabyte usage.

7. Granularity

The level of detail at which data is stored or processed. Finer granularity often increases the number of megabytes required.

8. Greedy Algorithm

An algorithm that makes the best immediate choice at each step. Greedy algorithms may reduce memory usage by limiting how many megabytes of data must be stored at once.

9. Ground Truth Data

Correct, labeled data used to train or evaluate AI systems. Ground truth datasets are stored in files measured in megabytes or larger units.

10. Growth Rate (Data)

The speed at which data size increases over time. In AI systems, a high data growth rate means storage needs measured in megabytes can expand quickly.

Letter H

1. Hard Disk Capacity

The total amount of data a hard disk can store. Capacity is measured in megabytes and larger units.

2. Hardware Acceleration

The use of specialized hardware to speed up AI processing. Acceleration often reduces how long megabytes of data stay in memory.

3. Hash Table

A data structure that stores information for fast lookup. Hash tables occupy memory measured in megabytes in large AI systems.

4. Hierarchical Storage

A storage design that uses multiple layers such as RAM, disk, and cloud. Each layer manages data measured in megabytes.

5. High-Dimensional Data

Data with many features or variables. High-dimensional datasets often require large numbers of megabytes.

6. Host Memory

Main system memory used by the CPU. Host memory stores AI data and models measured in megabytes.

7. Hybrid Storage

A combination of different storage types working together. Hybrid storage systems manage megabytes across multiple devices.

8. Hyperparameter Storage

Memory used to store configuration values for AI models. These settings are saved in files measured in megabytes.

9. Hyperscale Data

Extremely large datasets used by major AI systems. Hyperscale data is tracked from megabytes up to much larger units.

10. Heuristic Data

Information used by AI systems to guide decision-making. Heuristic data contributes to the overall data size in megabytes.

Letter I

1. Image Dataset Size

The total amount of storage required for image data. Size is measured in megabytes or more.

2. Inference Memory

The memory used when an AI model is making predictions. Inference memory usage is tracked in megabytes.

3. Input Buffer

A temporary area where incoming data is stored. Input buffers hold megabytes before processing begins.

4. Intermediate Data

Data produced during processing steps. Intermediate data can significantly increase memory usage in megabytes.

5. Index File

A file that helps locate data quickly. Index files use additional megabytes to improve performance.

6. Information Density

The amount of useful data stored within a given size. Higher density means more information per megabyte.

7. Initialization Data

Data loaded when an AI system starts. Initialization data occupies memory measured in megabytes.

8. In-Memory Processing

Processing data directly in RAM instead of storage. This approach uses large amounts of memory measured in megabytes.

9. Input Feature Size

The amount of data required to represent input features. Feature size affects how many megabytes are needed.

10. Instruction Cache

A small memory area that stores frequently used instructions. Instruction caches manage small but critical megabytes.

Letter J

1. Job Queue

A list of tasks waiting to be processed. Job queues may store task data measured in megabytes.

2. Joint Dataset

A dataset created by combining multiple sources. Joint datasets often increase total size in megabytes.

3. JSON Data Size

The amount of storage required for data stored in JSON format. JSON files can grow quickly in megabytes.

4. Jitter Buffer

A temporary storage area that smooths data flow. Jitter buffers store megabytes during real-time processing.

5. Job Scheduler

A system that decides when tasks run. Schedulers manage memory and data measured in megabytes.

6. Just-in-Time Processing

Processing data only when needed. This approach can reduce how many megabytes are stored at once.

7. Joint Memory Allocation

Memory shared across multiple AI tasks. Joint allocation must carefully manage available megabytes.

8. Java Bytecode Size

The storage size of compiled Java programs. Bytecode files occupy megabytes on disk.

9. Job Metadata

Information describing AI tasks. Metadata adds additional megabytes to total system storage.

10. Junction Storage Point

A logical link between storage locations. Junctions help organize data measured in megabytes.

Letter K

1. Kernel Memory

Memory reserved for core system operations. Kernel memory usage is tracked in megabytes.

2. Key-Value Store

A data storage method that pairs keys with values. Large key-value stores consume many megabytes.

3. Knowledge Base Size

The total amount of stored knowledge in an AI system. Size is measured in megabytes or larger units.

4. K-Means Dataset Size

The amount of data used in clustering algorithms. Dataset size affects memory usage in megabytes.

5. Keras Model Size

The storage required for AI models built with Keras. Model size is measured in megabytes.

6. Keyframe Data

Important frames selected from video data. Keyframe storage contributes to total megabyte usage.

7. Kernel Cache

A cache used by the operating system kernel. Kernel caches store frequently used data in megabytes.

8. Knowledge Graph Storage

Memory used to store relationships between data points. Knowledge graphs require significant megabytes.

9. Kinetic Data Stream

Continuously changing data from sensors or systems. These streams generate growing megabytes over time.

10. K-Nearest Neighbor Memory Usage

The memory required by nearest-neighbor algorithms. Memory use increases as datasets grow in megabytes.

Letter L

1. **Latency**
   The delay between requesting data and receiving it. Latency affects how quickly megabytes move through AI systems.
2. **Layer Output Size**
   The amount of data produced by a neural network layer. Output size is measured in megabytes during processing.
3. **Load Balancing**
   Distributing work across systems so no single device is overloaded. Balancing helps manage megabytes efficiently.
4. **Local Storage**
   Data stored on a device rather than the cloud. Local storage capacity is measured in megabytes.
5. **Log File Size**
   The amount of storage used by system logs. Logs can accumulate many megabytes over time.
6. **Loss History Data**
   Stored values showing how model error changes during training. Loss history consumes megabytes.
7. **Low-Precision Data**
   Data stored using fewer bits per value. Low-precision formats reduce megabyte usage.
8. **Labeled Dataset**
   Data that includes tags or labels for AI training. Labels increase total dataset size in megabytes.
9. **Linear Model Size**
   The storage required for a linear AI model. Size is measured in megabytes.
10. **Load Time**
    The time required to bring data or models into memory. Load time depends on megabytes involved.

Letter M

1. **Memory Allocation**
   Assigning a specific amount of memory for tasks. Allocation is tracked in megabytes.
2. **Memory Footprint**
   The total memory an AI program uses. Footprint is measured in megabytes.
3. **Metadata Size**
   The storage used by descriptive information about data. Metadata adds extra megabytes.
4. **Mini-Batch Size**
   The amount of data processed at once during training. Batch size affects megabyte usage.

5. **Model Checkpoint Size**
   The storage required for saved training states. Checkpoints often consume many megabytes.
6. **Model Compression**
   Reducing model size while preserving performance. Compression lowers megabytes required.
7. **Model Parameters**
   Values learned by an AI model. Parameter storage contributes to total megabytes.
8. **Memory Bandwidth**
   The rate at which memory transfers data. Bandwidth affects how fast megabytes move.
9. **Multimodal Dataset**
   Data combining text, images, audio, or video. Multimodal data uses large megabytes.
10. **Mutable Data**
    Data that changes during processing. Mutable data can increase temporary megabyte usage.

Letter N

1. **Network Bandwidth**
   The capacity of a network connection. Bandwidth controls how many megabytes can be transferred.
2. **Neural Network Size**
   The total storage required for a neural network. Size is measured in megabytes.
3. **Node Memory**
   Memory available on a computing node. Node memory limits megabytes per task.
4. **Normalization Data**
   Values used to scale data consistently. Normalization adds to dataset megabytes.
5. **Non-Volatile Memory**
   Memory that retains data without power. Capacity is measured in megabytes.
6. **Numerical Precision**
   The detail level of stored numbers. Higher precision increases megabytes.
7. **Noise Data**
   Unwanted or random information in datasets. Noise increases data size in megabytes.
8. **Neural Activation Size**
   Memory used to store neuron outputs. Activation size is measured in megabytes.
9. **Network Transfer Size**
   The amount of data sent across a network. Transfer size is tracked in megabytes.
10. **Node Cache**
    Temporary storage on a node for faster access. Cache size uses megabytes.

Letter O

1. **Object Storage**
   A storage method that manages data as objects. Capacity is measured in megabytes.

2. **Offline Dataset**
   Data stored locally rather than streamed. Offline datasets occupy megabytes.
3. **On-Device Storage**
   Storage located on the AI device itself. On-device capacity is measured in megabytes.
4. **Operational Memory**
   Memory used during active AI operations. Usage is tracked in megabytes.
5. **Optimization Data**
   Information used to improve model performance. Optimization data uses megabytes.
6. **Output Buffer**
   Temporary storage for results before delivery. Buffers hold megabytes.
7. **Overhead Data**
   Extra data required for system operation. Overhead increases total megabytes.
8. **Object Detection Output Size**
   The amount of data produced by detection models. Output size is measured in megabytes.
9. **Online Storage**
   Storage accessible via the internet. Online storage limits are measured in megabytes.
10. **Open Dataset Size**
   The storage footprint of publicly available datasets. Size is measured in megabytes.

Letter P

1. **Parameter Count**
   The total number of model values. Count correlates with megabytes required.
2. **Persistent Storage**
   Long-term storage that retains data. Capacity is measured in megabytes.
3. **Pipeline Buffer**
   Temporary storage between processing stages. Buffers manage megabytes in motion.
4. **Preprocessing Data**
   Data created while preparing datasets. Preprocessing adds megabytes.
5. **Precision Reduction**
   Lowering numeric detail to save space. Reduction decreases megabyte usage.
6. **Prediction Output Size**
   The amount of data produced by model predictions. Size is measured in megabytes.
7. **Primary Memory**
   Main system memory used for processing. Capacity is measured in megabytes.
8. **Processing Overhead**
   Extra resources needed during computation. Overhead increases megabyte usage.
9. **Profiling Data**
   Information collected to analyze performance. Profiling data uses megabytes.
10. **Paged Memory**
   Memory divided into fixed-size blocks. Paging manages megabytes efficiently.

Letter Q

1. **Quantization**
   A technique that reduces numerical precision to lower memory usage. Quantization helps AI models use fewer megabytes.
2. **Query Cache**
   Stored results from previous searches or requests. Query caches save megabytes by avoiding repeated computation.
3. **Query Latency**
   The time it takes to retrieve data after a request. Latency depends on how many megabytes must be accessed.
4. **Queue Buffer**
   A temporary holding area for data waiting to be processed. Buffers store megabytes in order.
5. **Quick Access Memory**
   Memory designed for fast retrieval. It handles megabytes needed immediately by AI tasks.
6. **Quantitative Dataset**
   Data made up of numerical values. These datasets are stored and measured in megabytes.
7. **Query Result Size**
   The amount of data returned from a query. Result size is measured in megabytes.
8. **Quorum Storage**
   A distributed storage method requiring agreement across systems. Data is replicated in megabytes.
9. **Quality Metrics Data**
   Information used to measure model performance. Metrics consume storage in megabytes.
10. **Quantized Model Size**
    The reduced size of an AI model after quantization. Size is typically measured in megabytes.

Letter R

1. **RAM Usage**
   The amount of active memory in use. RAM usage is tracked in megabytes.
2. **Read Throughput**
   The speed at which data is read from storage. Throughput affects how fast megabytes are accessed.
3. **Real-Time Processing**
   Processing data immediately as it arrives. Real-time systems manage megabytes continuously.
4. **Recursive Memory Use**
   Memory consumption during repeated function calls. Usage accumulates in megabytes.
5. **Redundant Storage**
   Extra copies of data kept for reliability. Redundancy increases total megabytes stored.
6. **Resource Allocation**
   Assigning system resources like memory and storage. Allocation is measured in megabytes.

7. **Runtime Memory**
   Memory required while a program is running. Runtime memory usage is tracked in megabytes.
8. **Raw Dataset Size**
   The size of unprocessed data. Raw datasets often require many megabytes.
9. **Read-Only Memory Footprint**
   The storage space used by non-modifiable data. Footprint is measured in megabytes.
10. **Retrieval Speed**
    How quickly stored data can be accessed. Speed depends on the number of megabytes involved.

Letter S

1. **Sample Size**
   The number of data examples used in AI training. Larger samples increase megabytes.
2. **Scalable Storage**
   Storage that grows with demand. Scalability supports increasing megabytes.
3. **Serialized Data Size**
   The storage size of data converted into a transferable format. Size is measured in megabytes.
4. **Shared Memory**
   Memory accessible by multiple processes. Shared memory usage is tracked in megabytes.
5. **Snapshot Size**
   The storage required for saved system states. Snapshots consume megabytes.
6. **Sparse Data Representation**
   A storage method that saves space when data contains many empty values. Sparsity reduces megabytes.
7. **Storage Capacity**
   The total amount of data a system can store. Capacity is measured in megabytes or more.
8. **Streaming Data Buffer**
   Temporary storage for incoming data streams. Buffers handle megabytes in motion.
9. **System Cache**
   Memory that stores frequently used data. Caches manage megabytes for faster access.
10. **Synchronization Data**
    Information used to keep systems aligned. Sync data adds to total megabytes.

Letter T

1. **Temporary Storage**
   Short-term storage used during processing. Temporary storage holds megabytes briefly.
2. **Tensor Size**
   The memory required to store multidimensional data structures. Tensor size is measured in megabytes.
3. **Throughput Rate**
   The amount of data processed per unit time. Rate is often described in megabytes per second.

4. **Training Dataset Size**

   The total amount of data used to train AI models. Size is measured in megabytes.

5. **Transfer Buffer**

   Temporary memory used during data movement. Buffers hold megabytes during transfer.

6. **Transactional Storage**

   Storage that ensures data consistency. Transactions add overhead measured in megabytes.

7. **Thread Memory Usage**

   Memory consumed by execution threads. Usage is tracked in megabytes.

8. **Token Storage Size**

   The memory required to store processed tokens. Token data uses megabytes.

9. **Time-Series Data Size**

   The storage footprint of data collected over time. Size increases in megabytes.

10. **Training Checkpoint Size**

    The storage required for saved training states. Checkpoints are measured in megabytes.

Letter U

1. **Unified Memory**

   A memory system shared between CPU and GPU. Unified memory manages data in megabytes efficiently across processors.

2. **Upload Size**

   The amount of data sent to storage or the cloud. Upload size is measured in megabytes.

3. **User Data Storage**

   Storage allocated for user-generated files. Capacity is tracked in megabytes.

4. **Utilization Rate**

   The percentage of memory or storage currently in use. Utilization reflects how many megabytes are occupied.

5. **Uncompressed Data Size**

   The size of data before compression. Uncompressed data often uses more megabytes.

6. **Update Payload**

   Data sent during software or model updates. Payload size is measured in megabytes.

7. **Uptime Storage Logs**

   Logs recorded while systems run continuously. Logs accumulate megabytes over time.

8. **Unified Dataset**

   A dataset combined from multiple sources. Size is measured in megabytes.

9. **User Session Memory**

   Memory allocated for active users. Session memory uses megabytes dynamically.

10. **Usage Quota**

    A storage limit set for users or systems. Quotas are defined in megabytes or larger units.

Letter V

1. **Validation Dataset Size**

   The amount of data used to evaluate AI models. Size is measured in megabytes.

2. **Vector Embedding Size**
   The memory required to store numerical representations of data. Size is measured in megabytes.
3. **Virtual Memory**
   A system that extends RAM using disk storage. Virtual memory is managed in megabytes.
4. **Volatile Memory**
   Memory that loses data when power is off. Capacity is measured in megabytes.
5. **Video Dataset Size**
   The storage required for video data. Video datasets consume many megabytes.
6. **Versioned Storage**
   Storage that keeps multiple file versions. Versioning increases megabyte usage.
7. **Vision Model Size**
   The memory footprint of computer vision models. Size is measured in megabytes.
8. **Vector Database Storage**
   Storage used for similarity search data. Vector databases consume large megabytes.
9. **Virtualized Storage**
   Storage abstracted from physical hardware. Capacity is tracked in megabytes.
10. **Volume Capacity**
    The total size of a storage volume. Capacity is measured in megabytes or more.

Letter W

1. **Weight Parameters**
   Learned values in AI models. Weight storage contributes to megabytes used.
2. **Working Memory**
   Memory actively used during processing. Working memory usage is measured in megabytes.
3. **Write Throughput**
   The speed at which data is written to storage. Throughput affects megabytes per second.
4. **Warm Cache**
   Cached data that is already loaded. Warm caches reduce repeated megabyte transfers.
5. **Workflow Data Size**
   The total data used across an AI workflow. Size is measured in megabytes.
6. **Web Dataset Size**
   The storage required for web-based data. Size is tracked in megabytes.
7. **Weight Compression**
   Reducing model weight size to save memory. Compression lowers megabytes used.
8. **Window Size (AI Context)**
   The amount of data processed at once. Window size affects memory megabytes.
9. **Writable Storage**
   Storage that allows data modification. Capacity is measured in megabytes.
10. **Workload Memory Demand**
    The memory required for tasks. Demand is expressed in megabytes.

Letter X

1. **X-Axis Data Size**
   Data stored along one dimension of a dataset. Size contributes to megabytes used.
2. **XML Data Size**
   The storage footprint of XML-formatted data. XML files often use many megabytes.
3. **XOR Encoding**
   A binary operation used in data processing. Encoded data occupies megabytes.
4. **Execution Context Size**
   Memory required during task execution. Size is measured in megabytes.
5. **External Dataset Size**
   The size of data sourced externally. External datasets add megabytes.
6. **Expanded Memory Use**
   Memory growth during processing. Expansion increases megabytes consumed.
7. **Experimental Dataset**
   Data used for testing AI models. Size is measured in megabytes.
8. **Extraction Buffer**
   Temporary storage during data extraction. Buffers store megabytes briefly.
9. **Extended Storage Capacity**
   Additional storage added to a system. Capacity is measured in megabytes.
10. **Explainability Data Size**
    Data used to explain AI decisions. Explainability outputs consume megabytes.

Letter Y

1. **Yield Data Size**
   The amount of useful output data produced. Yield is measured in megabytes.
2. **Yearly Data Growth**
   Annual increase in stored data. Growth is tracked in megabytes.
3. **YAML File Size**
   The storage footprint of YAML configuration files. Size is measured in megabytes.
4. **Y-Axis Feature Size**
   Feature data along a dataset dimension. Size contributes to megabytes.
5. **Young Generation Memory**
   Memory area for newly created data. Usage is measured in megabytes.
6. **Yield Optimization Data**
   Data used to improve output efficiency. Stored in megabytes.
7. **YourAIStudyBuddy Dataset Size**
   The total data used by AI study tools. Size is measured in megabytes.
8. **Yottabyte Reference Scale**
   A conceptual upper scale of data measurement. Used for comparison beyond megabytes.
9. **Yield Metrics Storage**
   Storage used for performance metrics. Metrics consume megabytes.
10. **Yoked Memory Allocation**
    Linked memory regions used together. Allocation is measured in megabytes.

Letter Z

1. **Zero-Copy Memory**
   A method that avoids duplicating data. Zero-copy reduces megabytes in motion.
2. **Zipped Dataset Size**
   The storage size after compression. Zipped files use fewer megabytes.
3. **Zettabyte Scale (Reference)**
   A large-scale data concept. Used to compare growth beyond megabytes.
4. **Zone-Based Storage**
   Storage divided into regions. Zones manage megabytes efficiently.
5. **Z-Score Normalization Data**
   Statistical values used in preprocessing. Data adds megabytes.
6. **Zero Padding**
   Adding placeholder data to inputs. Padding increases memory megabytes.
7. **Zoomed Feature Maps**
   Scaled representations in vision models. Stored in megabytes.
8. **Zonal Cache**
   Cache divided by region. Cache size is measured in megabytes.
9. **Zero-Day Model Update Size**
   The storage required for emergency updates. Size is measured in megabytes.
10. **Zipped Model Archive**
    Compressed AI model files. Archives reduce megabytes required.

Teacher Implementation Guide

Data: Fuel for Artificial Neurons

How Information Powers Intelligent Machines

Purpose of This Teacher Guide

This Teacher Implementation Guide is designed to assist educators in teaching the concepts presented in **Data: Fuel for Artificial Neurons**. The guide provides instructional strategies, classroom discussion ideas, activities, and assessment suggestions to help students understand how **data powers artificial intelligence systems**.

Artificial intelligence systems do not learn from intuition or experience in the same way humans do. Instead, they learn from **data**—the vast collections of information that allow machines to detect patterns, make predictions, and improve their performance over time.

In this book, students explore the journey of data from its origin in the real world to its role inside artificial neural networks. Along the way, they learn how data must be carefully collected, organized, and interpreted to ensure that AI systems behave accurately, fairly, and responsibly.

The goal of this course is to help students develop **data literacy**, an essential skill for the modern digital world. Students will learn not only how data powers intelligent systems but also why ethical data practices are necessary to protect individuals and societies.

Recommended Grade Levels

This curriculum is appropriate for:

- **Grades 8–12**
- STEM and computer science programs
- AI literacy courses
- Early college technology courses

Students do **not need programming experience** to understand the concepts presented in this book.

Course Duration Options

Teachers may implement this curriculum in multiple formats depending on instructional time.

Option 1 — Full Semester Course

16 weeks
1 chapter per week

Option 2 — Quarter Course

8 weeks
2 chapters per week

Option 3 — AI Literacy Unit

4–6 weeks
Selected chapters

Instructional Framework

Each chapter may be taught using the following instructional model.

1. Opening Question (10 minutes)

Begin the lesson with a question that encourages curiosity.

Examples:

• Where does the information used by AI come from?
• Can machines learn without data?
• What happens when data is incorrect or biased?

These questions help students connect their prior knowledge with the new material.

2. Concept Exploration (20–30 minutes)

Students read the chapter and identify key ideas.

Teachers may guide students to focus on:

• New vocabulary
• Important diagrams or examples
• Connections to real-world technology

Encourage students to summarize the main concept of the chapter in their own words.

3. Discussion and Analysis (15 minutes)

Teachers lead a class discussion exploring the implications of the chapter.

Discussion may include:

• How data shapes AI decision-making
• Why data quality matters
• Ethical responsibilities related to data collection

4. Hands-On Activity (15–20 minutes)

Students complete a worksheet, activity, or demonstration that reinforces the concept.

Possible activities include:

• Identifying patterns in datasets
• Comparing biased vs unbiased datasets
• Visualizing data using charts

5. Reflection (10 minutes)

Students write a brief reflection responding to questions such as:

• What new idea did you learn today?
• Why is data important for intelligent systems?
• What risks might occur if data is misused?

Course Learning Objectives

By the end of this course, students will be able to:

Explain what data is and why it is essential for artificial intelligence systems.

Describe how machines interpret numbers and patterns through artificial neurons.

Distinguish between structured and unstructured data.

Understand the role of training data and testing data in machine learning.

Explain how data preprocessing improves machine learning performance.

Analyze the importance of ethical data use and privacy protection.

Interpret data using charts, graphs, and visual tools.

Evaluate how data-driven systems influence modern technology.

Chapter Implementation Overview

Stage 1 — Understanding Data Foundations

Chapters 1–4

Focus: What data is and why it matters for AI.

Teacher goals:

• Introduce the concept of data as the foundation of AI
• Explain how machines interpret numbers and patterns
• Help students understand how poor data can produce misleading results

Suggested activities:

• Sorting data into categories
• Identifying patterns in simple datasets
• Discussing examples of biased data

Key discussion questions:

• Why do machines depend on data instead of experience?
• How can incorrect data create unfair AI systems?

Stage 2 — Data Sources and Formats

Chapters 5–7

Focus: Where data comes from and how machines interpret it.

Teacher goals:

• Explain how sensors, images, audio, and text generate data
• Compare structured vs unstructured data
• Show how neural networks process inputs

Suggested activities:

• Classifying different types of data sources
• Identifying examples of structured vs unstructured data
• Visualizing a simple neural network

Key discussion questions:

• How do machines convert real-world information into numbers?
• Why is unstructured data more difficult to analyze?

Stage 3 — Machine Learning with Data

Chapters 8–11

Focus: The role of datasets in training AI systems.

Teacher goals:

• Explain training data and testing data
• Introduce the concept of big data ecosystems
• Demonstrate how preprocessing improves learning

Suggested activities:

• Training/testing dataset simulation
• Feature identification exercise
• Data cleaning demonstration

Key discussion questions:

• Why must AI systems be tested after training?
• How does data preparation improve machine learning results?

Stage 4 — Data Responsibility and Future Technologies

Chapters 12–16

Focus: Ethics, visualization, real-world applications, and future trends.

Teacher goals:

• Teach responsible data use and privacy awareness
• Introduce data visualization techniques
• Explore emerging trends such as synthetic data

Suggested activities:

- Ethical debate on data privacy
- Creating charts from sample datasets
- Research projects on real-world AI systems

Key discussion questions:

- Who owns the data used by AI systems?
- How should societies regulate the use of data?

Assessment Suggestions

Teachers may evaluate student understanding using several assessment methods.

Formative Assessments

- Chapter quizzes
- Reflection responses
- Worksheets and class discussions
- Group activities

Summative Assessments

- Research reports on data-driven technologies
- Presentations on ethical data practices
- Final project exploring AI applications

Final Project Idea

Students may complete a project titled:

"Designing an AI System Powered by Data."

Students explain:

- What problem their AI system would solve
- What types of data it would require
- How the data would be collected and processed
- How they would protect privacy and avoid bias

This project helps students apply both **technical and ethical knowledge**.

Encouraging Data Literacy

Understanding data is one of the most important skills of the modern era.

Students who understand data can:

• Interpret information critically
• Recognize misleading statistics
• Evaluate AI systems responsibly

This course helps students build the foundation needed to navigate a world increasingly shaped by data-driven technologies.

Final Note to Educators

Artificial intelligence systems depend on data just as engines depend on fuel.
Without high-quality data, even the most advanced algorithms cannot function effectively.

By helping students understand how data powers artificial neurons, educators prepare them to participate thoughtfully in a future where **information and intelligence are deeply connected**.

Through this book, students gain not only knowledge about AI but also a deeper appreciation for the role data plays in shaping technology, society, and human understanding.